Leadership Beyond Words

Dale Harbison Carnegie (24 November 1888–1 November 1955) was an American writer and lecturer and the developer of famous courses in self-improvement, salesmanship, corporate training, public speaking and interpersonal skills. Born into poverty on a farm in Missouri, he was the author of the bestselling *How to Win Friends and Influence People* (1936), *How to Stop Worrying and Start Living* (1948) and many more self-help books.

Leadership Beyond Words

Dale Carnegie's *Legacy* for *Today's World*

Dale Carnegie

Published by
Rupa Publications India Pvt. Ltd 2024
7/16, Ansari Road, Daryaganj
New Delhi 110002

Sales centres:
Bengaluru Chennai
Hyderabad Jaipur Kathmandu
Kolkata Mumbai Prayagraj

Edition copyright © Rupa Publications India Pvt. Ltd 2024

All rights reserved.
No part of this publication may be reproduced, transmitted,
or stored in a retrieval system, in any form or by any means,
electronic, mechanical, photocopying, recording or otherwise, without
the prior permission of the publisher.

P-ISBN: 978-93-5702-835-6
E-ISBN: 978-93-5702-887-5

Second impression 2024

10 9 8 7 6 5 4 3 2

Printed in India

This book is sold subject to the condition that it shall not, by way of
trade or otherwise, be lent, resold, hired out, or otherwise circulated,
without the publisher's prior consent, in any form of binding or
cover other than that in which it is published.

CONTENTS

1. Finding the Leader in You — 7
2. Speak Effectively, the Quick and Easy Way — 16
3. Setting Goals — 29
4. Focus and Discipline — 41
5. Increase Courage and Self-Confidence — 52
6. Acquiring the Basic Skills — 66
7. Applying What You Have Learned — 77
8. Creating A Positive Mental Attitude — 86
9. Remember that no one Ever Kicks A Dead Dog — 90
10. The Big Secret of Dealing With People — 94
11. Make A Good First Impression — 104
12. Teaming Up for Tomorrow — 113
13. How to Encourage People — 126
14. A Law that Will Outlaw Many of Your Worries — 130
15. Right Thinking and Personality — 135
16. How to Criticize—and Not Be Hated for it — 141
17. If You Don't Do this, You Are Headed for Trouble — 146
18. Making it Happen — 150

1

FINDING THE LEADER IN YOU

Fred Wilpon is the president of the New York Mets baseball team. One afternoon, Wilpon was leading a group of school children on a tour of Shea Stadium. He let them stand behind home plate. He took them into the team dugouts. He walked them through the private passage to the clubhouse. As the final stop on his tour, Wilpon wanted to take the students into the stadium bull pen, where the pitchers warm up.

But right outside the bull pen gate, the group was stopped by a uniformed security guard.

'The bull pen isn't open to the public,' the guard told Wilpon, obviously unaware of who he was. 'I'm sorry, but you can't go out there.'

Now, Fred Wilpon certainly had the power to get what he wanted right then and there. He could have berated the poor security guard for failing to recognize such an important person as himself. With a dramatic flourish, Wilpon could have whipped out his top-level security pass and shown the wide-eyed children how much weight he carried at Shea.

Wilpon did none of that. He led the students to the far side of the stadium and took them into the bull pen through another gate.

Why did he bother to do that? Wilpon didn't want to

embarrass the security guard. The man, after all, was doing his job and doing it well. Later that afternoon, Wilpon even sent off a handwritten note, thanking the guard for showing such concern.

Had Wilpon chosen instead to yell or cause a scene, the guard might well have ended up feeling resentful, and no doubt his work would have suffered as a result. Wilpon's gentle approach made infinitely more sense. The guard felt great about the compliment. And you can bet he'll recognize Wilpon the next time the two of them happen to meet.

Fred Wilpon is a leader and not just because of the title he holds or the salary he earns. What makes him a leader of men and women is how he has learned to interact.

IMPORTANCE OF BEING A PEOPLE PERSON

In the past, people in the business world didn't give much thought to the true meaning of leadership. The boss was the boss, and he was in charge. Period. End of discussion.

Well-run companies—no one ever spoke about 'well-led companies'—were the ones that operated in almost military style. Orders were delivered from above and passed down through the ranks.

Remember Mr Dithers from the *Blondie* comic strip? *'BUM-STEAD!'* he would scream, and young Dagwood would come rushing into the boss's office like a frightened puppy. Lots of real-life companies operated that way for years. The companies that weren't run like army platoons were barely run at all. They just puttered along as they always had, secure in some little niche of a market that hadn't been challenged for years. The message from above was always, 'If it ain't broke, why fix it?'

The people who had responsibility sat in their offices and managed what they could. That's what they were expected to do—to 'manage'. Maybe they steered the organizations a few degrees to the left or a few degrees to the right. Usually, they tried to deal with whatever obvious problems presented themselves, and then they called it a day.

Back when the world was a simpler place, management like this was fine. Rarely visionary, but fine, as life rolled predictably along.

But mere management simply isn't enough anymore. The world is too unpredictable, too volatile, too fast-moving for such an uninspired approach. What's needed now is something much deeper than old-fashioned business management. What's needed is *leadership, to help people achieve what they are capable of, to establish a vision for the future, to encourage, to coach and to mentor, and to establish and maintain successful relationships.*

'Back when businesses operated in a more stable environment, management skills were sufficient,' says Harvard Business School Professor John Quelch. 'But when the business environment becomes volatile, when the waters are uncharted, when your mission requires greater flexibility than you ever imagined it would—that's when leadership skills become critical.'

'The change is already taking place, and I'm not sure all organizations are ready for it,' says Bill Makahilahila, Director of Human Resources at SGS-Thomson Microelectronics, Inc., a leading semiconductor manufacturer. 'The position called "manager" may not exist too much longer, and the concept of "leadership" will be redefined. Companies today are going through that struggle. They are realizing, as they begin to downsize their operations and reach for greater productivity, that facilitative skills are going to be primary. Good communication, interpersonal skills, the ability to coach, model, and build teams—all of that requires more and better leaders.

'You can't do it by directive anymore. It has to be by

influence. It takes real "people skills".'

BALANCE YOUR WORK LIFE AND SOCIAL LIFE

Many people still have a narrow understanding of what leadership really is. You say, 'leader' and they think *general, president, prime minister or chairman of the board*. Obviously, people in those exalted positions are expected to lead, an expectation they meet with varying levels of success. But the fact of the matter is that leadership does not begin and end at the very top. It is every bit as important, perhaps more important, in the places most of us live and work.

Organizing a small work team, energizing an office support staff, keeping things happy at home—those are the front lines of leadership. Leadership is never easy. But thankfully, something else is also true: every one of us has the potential to be a leader every day.

The team facilitator, the middle manager, the account executive, the customer-service operator, the person who works in the mail room—just about anyone who ever comes in contact with others has good reason to learn how to lead.

To an enormous degree their leadership skills will determine how much success they achieve and how happy they will be. Not just at work, either. Families, charity groups, sports teams, civic associations, social clubs, you name it—every one of those organizations has a tremendous need for dynamic leadership.

Steve Jobs and Steve Wozniak were a couple of blue-jeans-wearing kids from California, ages twenty-one and twenty-six. They weren't rich, they had absolutely no business training, and they were hoping to get started in an industry that barely existed at the time.

The year was 1976, before most people ever thought about buying computers for their homes. In those days the entire home-computer business added up to just a few brainy hobbyists, the original 'computer nerds'. So when Jobs and Wozniak scraped together thirteen hundred dollars by selling a van and two calculators and opened Apple Computer, Inc., in Job's garage, the odds against their smashing success seemed awfully long.

But these two young entrepreneurs had a vision, a clear idea of what they believed they could achieve. 'Computers aren't just for nerds anymore,' they announced. 'Computers are going to be the bicycle of the mind. Low-cost computers are for everyone.'

From day one the Apple founders kept their vision intact, and they communicated it at every turn. They hired people who understood the vision and let them share in its rewards. They lived and breathed and talked the vision. Even when the company got stalled—when the retailers said no thank you, when the manufacturing people said no way, when the bankers said no more—Apple's visionary leaders never backed down.

Eventually the world came around. Six years after Apple's founding, the company was selling 650,000 personal computers a year. Wozniak and Jobs were dynamic personal leaders, years ahead of their time.

It's not just new organizations, however, that need visionary leadership. In the early 1980s, Corning, Incorporated, was caught in a terrible squeeze. The Corning name still meant something in kitchenware, but that name was being seriously undermined. The company's manufacturing technology was outmoded. Its market share was down. Corning customers were defecting by the thousands to foreign firms. And the company's stodgy management didn't seem to have a clue.

That's when Chairman James R. Houghton concluded that Corning needed a whole new vision, and he proposed one.

Recalls Houghton, "We had an outside consultant who was working with me and my new team as our resident shrink. He was really a facilitator, a wonderful guy who kept hammering on the quality issue as something we had to get into.

'We were in one of those terrible group meetings, and everybody was very depressed. I got up and announced that we were going to spend about ten million bucks that we didn't have. We were going to set up our own quality institute. We were going to get going on this.

'There were a lot of different things that put me over the top. But I am fast to admit, I just had a gut feeling that it was right. I had no idea of the implications, none, and how important it would be.'

Houghton knew that Corning had to improve the quality of its manufacturing and had to speed up delivery time. What the chairman did was take a risk. He sought advice from the best experts in the world—his own employees. Not just the manager and the company engineers. Houghton brought in the line employees too. He put a representative team together and told them to redesign Corning's entire manufacturing process—if that's what it took to bring the company around.

The answer, the team decided after six months of work, was to redesign certain plants to reduce defects on the assembly line and make the machines faster to retool. The teams also reorganized the way Corning kept its inventories to get faster turnaround. The results were astounding. When Houghton launched these changes, irregularities in a new fiber-optics coating process were running eight hundred parts per million. Four years later that measure fell to zero. In two more years delivery time was cut from weeks to days, and in the space of four years Corning's return on equity nearly doubled. Houghton's vision had literally turned the company around.

Business theorists Warren Bennis and Burt Nanus have studied hundreds of successful organizations, large and small, focusing on the way in which they are led. 'A leader,' the two men write, 'must first have developed a mental image of a possible and desirable future state of the organization. This image, which we call a vision, may be as vague as a dream or as precise as a goal or a mission statement.' 'The critical point,' Bennis and Nanus explain, 'is that a vision articulates a view of a realistic, credible, attractive future for the organization, a condition that is better in some important ways than what now exists.'

SINCERITY MAKES DIFFERENCE

Leaders ask: where is this work team heading? What does this division stand for? Who are we trying to serve? How can we improve the quality of our work? The specific answers will be as different as the people being led, as different as the leaders themselves. What's most important is that the questions are asked.

There is no one correct way to lead, and talented leaders come in many personality types. They are loud or quiet, funny or severe, tough or gentle, boisterous or shy. They come from all ages, any race, both sexes and every kind of group there is.

The idea isn't just to identify the most successful leader you can find and then slavishly model yourself after him or her. That strategy is doomed from the start. You are unlikely ever to rise above a poor imitation of the person you are pretending to be. The leadership techniques that will work best for you are the ones you nurture inside.

A leader establishes standards and then sticks to them. Douglas A. Warner III, for instance, has always insisted on what he calls 'full transparency'.

'When you come in to make a proposal to me,' says Warner, president of J.P. Morgan & Co., Incorporated, 'assume that everything that you just told me appears tomorrow on the front page of the *Wall Street Journal*. Are you going to be proud to have handled this transaction or handled this situation in the way you just recommended, assuming full transparency? If the answer to that is no, then we're going to stop right here and examine what the problem is.' That is a mark of leadership.

Well-focused, self-confident leadership like that is what turns a vision into reality. Just ask Mother Teresa. She was a young Catholic nun, teaching high school in an upper-middle-class section of Calcutta. But she kept looking out the window and seeing the lepers on the street. 'I saw fear in their eyes,' she said. 'The fear they would never be loved, the fear they would never get adequate medical attention.'

She could not shake that fear out of her mind. She knew she had to leave the security of the convent, go out into the streets and set up homes of peace for the lepers of India. Over the years to come, Mother Teresa and her Missionaries of Charity have cared for 149,000 people with leprosy, dispensing medical attention and unconditional love.

One December day, after addressing the United Nations, Mother Teresa went to visit a maximum-security prison in upstate New York. While inside she spoke with four inmates who had AIDS. She knew at once that these were the lepers of today.

She got back to New York City on the Monday before Christmas, and she went straight to City Hall to see Mayor Edward Koch. She asked the mayor if he would telephone the governor, Mario Cuomo. 'Governor,' she said, after Koch handed her the phone, 'I'm just back from Sing Sing, and four prisoners there have AIDS. I'd like to open up an AIDS center.

Would you mind releasing those four prisoners to me? I'd like them to be the first four in the AIDS center.'

'Well, Mother,' Cuomo said, 'we have forty-three cases of AIDS in the state prison system. I'll release all forty-three to you.'

'Okay,' she said. 'I'd like to start with just the four. Now let me tell you about the building I have in mind. Would you like to pay for it?'

'Okay,' Cuomo agreed, bowled over by this woman's intensity.

Then Mother Teresa turned to Mayor Koch, and she said to him, 'Today is Monday. I'd like to open this on Wednesday. We're going to need some permits cleared. Could you please arrange those?'

Koch just looked at this tiny woman standing in his office and shook his head back and forth. 'As long as you don't make me wash the floors,' the mayor said.

POINTS TO REMEMBER

1. Redefining the term 'leadership'.
2. Value of people skills in a leader.
3. Answers don't matter as much as questions do.

2

SPEAK EFFECTIVELY, THE QUICK AND EASY WAY

'It is often dangerous to rush into battle without pausing for preparation or waiting for recruits.'

I seldom watch television in the daytime. But a friend recently asked me to listen to an afternoon show that was directed primarily to housewives. It enjoyed a very high rating, and my friend wanted me to listen because he thought the audience participation part of the show would interest me. It certainly did. I watched it several times, fascinated by the way the master of ceremonies succeeded in getting people in the audience to make talks in a way that caught and held my attention. These people were obviously not professional speakers. They had never been trained in the art of communication. Some of them used poor grammar and mispronounced words. But all of them were interesting. When they started to talk, they seemed to lose all fear of being on camera and they held the attention of the audience.

Why was this? I know the answer because I have been employing the techniques used in this program for many years. These people, plain, ordinary men and women, were holding the attention of viewers all over the country; they were talking about themselves, about their most embarrassing moments, their most pleasant memory or how they met their wives or husbands. They were not thinking of introduction, body and conclusion. They were not concerned with their diction or their sentence structure. Yet they were getting the final seal of approval from the audience—complete attention in what they had to say. This is dramatic proof of what to me is the first of three cardinal rules for a quick and easy way to learn to speak in public:

FIRST
Speak About Something You Have Earned the Right to Talk About Through Experience or Study

The men and women whose live flesh-and-blood stories made that television program interesting were talking from their own personal experience. They were talking about something they knew. Consider what a dull program would have resulted if they had been asked to define communism or to describe the organizational structure of the United Nations. Yet that is precisely the mistake that countless speakers make at countless meetings and banquets. They decide they must talk about subjects of which they have little or no personal knowledge and to which they have devoted little or no attention. They pick a subject like 'Patriotism', or 'Democracy', or 'Justice', and then, after a few hours of frantic searching through a book of quotations or a speaker's handbook for all occasions, they hurriedly throw together some generalizations vaguely remembered from a political science course they once took in college, and proceed to give a talk distinguished for nothing other than its length. It never occurs to these speakers that the audience might be interested in factual material bringing these high-flown concepts down to earth.

At an area meeting of Dale Carnegie instructors in the Conrad Hilton Hotel in Chicago some years ago, a student speaker started like this, 'Liberty, Equality, Fraternity. These are the mightiest ideas in the dictionary of mankind. Without liberty, life is not worth living. Imagine what existence would be like if your freedom of action would be restricted on all sides.'

That is as far as he got, because he was wisely stopped by the instructor, who then asked him why he believed what he was saying. He was asked whether he had any proof or personal experience to back up what he had just told us. Then he gave us an amazing story.

He had been a French underground fighter. He told us of the indignities he and his family suffered under Nazi rule. He described in vivid language how he escaped from the secret police and how he finally made his way to America. He ended by saying, 'When I walked down Michigan Avenue to this hotel today, I was free to come or go, as I wished. I passed a policeman and he took no notice of me. I walked into this hotel without having to present an identification card, and when this meeting is over, I can go anywhere in Chicago I choose to go. Believe me, freedom is worth fighting for.' He received a standing ovation from that audience.

TELL US WHAT LIFE HAS TAUGHT YOU

Speakers who talk about what life has taught them never fail to keep the attention of their listeners. I know from experience that speakers are not easily persuaded to accept this point of view—they avoid using personal experiences as too trivial and too restrictive. They would rather soar into the realms of general ideas and philosophical principles, where unfortunately the air is too rarefied for ordinary mortals to breathe. They give us editorials when we are hungry for the news. None of us is averse to listening to editorials, when they are given by a man who has earned the right to editorialize—an editor or publisher of a newspaper. The point, though, is this: speak on what life has taught you and I will be your devoted listener. It was said of Emerson that he was always willing to listen to any man, no matter how humble his station, because he felt he could learn something from every man he met. I have listened to more adult talks, perhaps, than any other man west of the Iron Curtain, and I can truthfully say that I have never heard a boring talk when the speaker related what life had taught him, no matter how slight or trivial the lesson may have been.

To illustrate: some years ago, one of our instructors conducted a course in public speaking for the senior officers of New York City banks. Naturally, the members of such a group, having many demands upon their time, frequently found it difficult to prepare adequately or to do what they conceived of as preparing. All their lives they had been thinking their own individual thoughts, nurturing their own personal convictions, seeing things from their own distinctive angles, living their own original experiences. They had spent forty years storing up material for talks. But it was hard for some of them to realize that.

One Friday, a certain gentleman connected with an uptown bank—for our purposes we shall designate him as Mr Jackson—found four-thirty had arrived, and what was he to talk about? He walked out of his office, bought a copy of *Forbes' Magazine* at a newsstand, and in the subway coming down to the Federal Reserve Bank where the class met, he read an article entitled, 'You Have Only Ten Years to Succeed'. He read it, not because he was interested in the article especially, but because he had to speak on something to fill his quota of time.

An hour later, he stood up and attempted to talk

convincingly and interestingly on the contents of this article.

What was the result, the inevitable result?

He had not digested, had not assimilated what he was trying to say. 'Trying to say'—that expresses it precisely. He was *trying*. There was no real message in him seeking for an outlet; and his whole manner and tone revealed it unmistakably. How could he expect the audience to be any more impressed than he himself was? He kept referring to the article, saying the author said so and so. There was a surfeit of *Forbes' Magazine* in it, but regrettably little of Mr Jackson.

After he finished his talk, the instructor said, 'Mr Jackson, we are not interested in this shadowy personality who wrote that article. He is not here. We can't see him. But we are interested in you and your ideas. Tell us what you think, personally, not what somebody else said. Put more of Mr Jackson in this. Would you take this same subject next week? Read this article again, and ask yourself whether you agree with the author or not. If you do, illustrate the points of agreement with observations from your own experience. If you don't agree with him, tell us why. Let this article be the starting point from which to launch your own talk.'

Mr Jackson reread the article and concluded that he did not agree with the author at all. He searched his memory for examples to prove his points of disagreement. He developed and expanded his ideas with details from his own experience as a bank executive. He came back the next week and gave a talk that was full of his own convictions, based on his own background. Instead of a warmed-over magazine article, he gave us ore from his own mine, currency coined in his own mint. I leave it to you to decide which talk made a stronger impact on the class.

LOOK FOR TOPICS IN YOUR BACKGROUND

Once a group of our instructors were asked to write on a slip of paper what they considered was the biggest problem they had with beginning speakers. When the slips were tallied, it was found that 'getting beginners to talk on the right topic' was the problem most frequently encountered in early sessions of my course.

What is the right topic? You can be sure you have the right topic for you if you have lived with it, made it your own through experience and reflection. How do you find topics? By dipping into your memory and searching your background for those significant aspects of your life that made a vivid impression on you. Several years ago, we made a survey of topics that held the attention of listeners in our classes. We found that the topics most approved by the audience were concerned with certain fairly defined areas of one's background:

Early Years and Upbringing. Topics that deal with the family, childhood memories, schooldays, invariably get attention, because most of us are interested in the way other people met and overcame obstacles in the environment in which they were reared.

Whenever possible, work into your talks illustrations and examples from your early years. The popularity of plays, movies and stories that deal with the subject of meeting the challenges of the world in one's early years attests to the value of this area for subject matter of talks. But how can you be sure anyone will be interested in what happened to you when you were young? There's one test. If something stands out vividly in your memory after many years have gone by, that almost guarantees that it will be of interest to an audience.

Early Struggles to Get Ahead. This is an area rich in human interest. Here again the attention of a group can be held by recounting your first attempts to make your mark on the world.

How did you get into a particular job or profession? What twist of circumstances accounted for your career? Tell us about your setbacks, your hopes, your triumphs when you were establishing yourself in the competitive world. A real-life picture of almost anyone's life—if told modestly—is almost surefire material.

Hobbies and Recreation. Topics in this area are based on personal choice and, as such, are subjects that command attention. You can't go wrong talking about something you do out of sheer enjoyment. Your natural enthusiasm for your particular hobby will help get this topic across to any audience.

Special Areas of Knowledge. Many years of working in the same field have made you an expert in your line of endeavor. You can be certain of respectful attention if you discuss aspects of your job or profession based on years of experience or study.

Unusual Experiences. Have you ever met a great man? Were you under fire during the war? Have you gone through a spiritual crisis in your life? These are experiences that make the best kind of speech material.

Beliefs and Convictions. Perhaps you have given a great deal of time and effort to thinking about your position on vital subjects confronting the world today. If you have devoted many hours to the study of issues of importance, you have earned the right to talk about them. But when you do, be certain that you give specific instances for your convictions. Audiences do not relish a talk filled with generalizations. Please don't consider the casual reading of a few newspaper articles sufficient preparation to talk on these topics. If you know little more about a subject than the people in your audience, it is best to avoid it. On the other hand, if you have devoted years of study to some subject, it is undoubtedly a topic that is made to order for you. By all means, use it.

◆

The preparation of a talk does not consist merely in getting some mechanical words down on paper, or in memorizing a series of phrases. It does not consist in lifting ideas secondhand from some hastily read book or newspaper article. But it does consist in digging deep into your mind and heart and bringing forth some of the essential convictions that life has stored there. Never doubt that the material is there. It is! Rich stores of it, waiting for you to discover it. Do not spurn such material as too personal, too slight for an audience to hear. I have been highly entertained and deeply moved by such talks, more entertained and more moved than I have been by many professional speakers.

Only by talking about something you have earned the right to talk about will you be able to fulfill the second requirement for learning to speak in public quickly and easily. Here it is:

SECOND
Be Sure You Are Excited About Your Subject

Not all topics that you and I have earned the right to talk about make us excited. For instance, as a do-it-yourself devotee, I certainly am qualified to talk about washing dishes. But somehow or other I can't get excited about this topic. As a matter of fact, I would rather forget about it altogether. Yet I have heard housewives—household executives, that is—give superb talks about this same subject. They have somehow aroused within themselves such a fury of indignation about the eternal task of washing dishes, or they have developed such ingenious methods of getting around this disagreeable chore, that they have become really excited about it. As a consequence, they have been able to talk effectively about this subject of washing dishes. Here is a question that will help you determine the suitability of topics you feel qualified to discuss in public:

if someone stood up and directly opposed your point of view, would you be impelled to speak with conviction and earnestness in defense of your position? If you would, you have the right subject for you.

Recently, I came across some notes I had written in 1926 after I had visited the Seventh Session of the League of Nations in Geneva, Switzerland. Here is a paragraph, 'After three or four lifeless speakers read their manuscripts, Sir George Foster of Canada took the floor. With immense satisfaction I noted that he had no papers or notes of any kind. He gestured almost constantly. His heart was in what he was saying. He had something he very much wanted to get across. The fact that he was earnestly trying to convey to the audience certain convictions that he cherished in his own heart was as plain as Lake Geneva outside the windows. Principles I have been advocating in my teaching were beautifully illustrated in that talk.'

I often recall that speech by Sir George. He was sincere; he was earnest. Only by choosing topics which are felt by the heart as well as thought out by the mind will this sincerity be made manifest. Bishop Fulton J. Sheen, one of America's most dynamic speakers, learned this lesson early in life.

'I was chosen for the debating team in college,' he wrote in his book, *Life Is Worth Living*, 'and the night before the Notre Dame debate, our professor of debating called me to his office and scolded me.

'"You are absolutely rotten. We have never had anybody in the history of this college who was a worse speaker than yourself."

'"Well" I said, trying to justify myself, "if I am so rotten why did you pick me for the team?"

'"Because," he answered, "you can think; not because you can talk. Get over in that corner. Take a paragraph of your speech and go through it." I repeated a paragraph over and over again for an hour, at the end of which he said, "Do you see any mistake in that?" "No." Again an hour and a half, two hours, two and a half hours, at the end of which I was exhausted. He said, "Do you still not see what is wrong?"

"'Being naturally quick, after two hours and a half, I caught on. I said, "Yes, I am not sincere. I am not myself. I do not talk as if I meant it."'

At this point, Bishop Sheen learned a lesson he always remembered: *he put himself into his talk*. He became excited about his subject matter. Only then the wise professor said, 'Now, you are ready to speak!'

When a member of one of our classes says, 'I don't get excited about anything, I lead a humdrum sort of life,' our instructors are trained to ask him what he does in his spare time. One goes to the movies, another bowls and another cultivates roses. One man told his instructor that he collected books of matches. As the instructor continued to question him about this unusual hobby, he gradually became animated. Soon he was using gestures as he described the cabinets in which he stored his collection. He told his instructor that he had match books from almost every country in the world. When he became excited about his favorite topic, the instructor stopped him. 'Why don't you tell us about this subject? It sounds fascinating to me.' He said that he didn't think anyone would be interested! Here was a man who had spent years in pursuit of a hobby that was almost a passion with him; yet he was negative about its value as a topic to speak about. This instructor assured this man that the only way to gauge the interest value of a subject was to ask yourself how interested you are in it. He talked that night with all the fervour of the true collector, and I heard later that he gained a certain amount of local recognition by going to various luncheon clubs and talking about match book collecting.

This illustration leads directly to the third guiding principle for those who want a quick and easy way to learn to speak in public.

THIRD
Be Eager to Share Your Talk with Your Listeners

There are three factors in every speaking situation: the speaker, the speech or the message and the audience. The first two rules in this chapter dealt with the interrelationships of the speaker to a speech. Up to this point there is no speaking situation. Only when the speaker relates his talk to a living audience will the speaking situation come to life. The talk may be well prepared; it may concern a topic which the speaker is excited about; but for complete success, another factor must enter into his delivery of the talk. He must make his listeners feel that what he has to say is important to them. He must not only be excited about his topic, but he must be eager to transfer this excitement to his listeners. In every public speaker of note in the history of eloquence, there has been this unmistakable quality of salesmanship, evangelism, call it what you will. The effective speaker earnestly desires his listeners to feel what he feels, to agree with his point of view, to do what he thinks is right for them to do and to enjoy and relive his experience with him. He is audience-centred and not self-centred. He knows that the success or failure of his talk is not for him to decide—it will be decided in the minds and hearts of his hearers.

I trained a number of men in the New York City Chapter of the American Institute of Banking to speak during a thrift campaign. One of the men in particular wasn't getting across to his audience. The first step in helping that man was to fire up his mind and heart with zeal for his subject. I told him to go off by himself and to think over this subject until he became enthusiastic about it. I asked him to remember that the Probate Court Records in New York show that more than 85 per cent of the people leave nothing at all at death; that only 3.3 per cent leave $10,000 or over. He was to keep constantly in mind that he was not asking people to do him a favour or something that they could not afford to do. He was to say to himself, 'I am preparing these people to have meat and bread and clothes and comfort in their old age, and to leave their wives and children secure.' He had to remember he was going out to perform a great social service. In short, he had to be a crusader.

He thought over these facts. He burned them into his mind. He aroused his own interest, stirred his own enthusiasm and came to feel that he, indeed, had a mission. Then, when he went out to talk, there was a ring to his words that carried conviction. He sold his listeners on the benefits of thrift because he had an eager desire to help people. He was no longer just a speaker armed with facts; he was a missionary seeking converts to a worthwhile cause.

At one time in my teaching career, I relied considerably on the textbook rules of public speaking. In doing this I was merely reflecting some of the bad habits that had been instilled into me by teachers who had not broken away from the stilted mechanics of elocution.

I shall never forget my first lesson in speaking. I was taught to let my arm hang loosely at my side, with the palm turned to the rear, fingers half-closed and thumb touching my leg. I was drilled to bring the arm up in a picturesque curve, to give the wrist a classical turn, and then to unfold the forefinger first, the second finger next and the little finger last. When the whole aesthetic and ornamental movement had been executed, the arm was to retrace the course of the curve and rest again by the side of the leg. The whole performance was wooden and affected. There was nothing sensible or honest about it.

My instructor made no attempt to get me to put my own individuality into my speaking; no attempt to have me speak like a normal, living human being conversing in an energetic manner with my audience.

Contrast this mechanistic approach to speech training with the three primary rules I have been discussing in this chapter. They are the basis of my entire approach to training in effective speaking. You will come across them again and again in this book.

POINTS TO REMEMBER

1. Make your speech authentic and relatable by speaking about your personal experiences.
2. Three factors of public speaking: speaker, speech and audience.
3. Enthusiasm is contagious. Be excited about your subject and the crowd will be too.

3

SETTING GOALS

Mary Lou Retton was just a high-school sophomore from West Virginia, a state that had never once produced a world-class gymnast.

'I was a nobody,' she says, 'and I was number one in the state.' She was a tiny fourteen-year-old, performing at a competition in Reno, Nevada. That's the day the great Bela Karolyi, the Romanian gymnastics coach who had guided Nadia Comaneci to Olympic gold, walked up behind Mary Lou.

'He was the king of gymnastics,' Retton recalls. 'He came up to me. He tapped me on the shoulder. He's a big man—six-three or six-four. He came up to me and said, "Mary Lou," in that deep Romanian accent. "You come to me, and I will make you Olympic champion."'

The first thought that went racing through Retton's mind was, 'Yeah, right. No way.'

But of all the gymnasts in that Nevada arena, Bela Karolyi had noticed her. 'So we sat down, and we talked,' Retton remembers. 'He talked with my parents and said, "Listen, there's no guarantee that Mary Lou will even make the Olympic team, but I think she's got the material that it takes."'

What a goal that was! Since early childhood she had harboured dreams about one day performing in the Olympics.

But hearing the words come out of the great man's mouth—as far as Retton was concerned, that set the goal in stone.

'It was a very big risk for me,' she says. 'I was going to be moving away from my family and my friends, living with a family I had never met before, training with girls I didn't know. It pumped me up so much. I was scared. I didn't know what to expect. But I was excited too. This man wanted to train me. Little me, from Fairmont, West Virginia. I had been picked out.'

And she wasn't about to let Karolyi down. It was two and a half years later that Mary Lou Retton, after a pair of perfect tens, won the Olympic gold medal in gymnastics for America—and with it a place in the hearts of people everywhere.

AIM, AND THEN SHOOT

Goals give us something to shoot for. They keep our efforts focused. They allow us to measure our success.

So set goals—goals that are challenging but also realistic, goals that are clear and measurable, goals for the short term and goals for the long term.

When you reach one goal, take a second to pat yourself on the back. Then move on to the next goal, emboldened, strengthened, energized by what you've already achieved.

Eugene Lang, a New York City philanthropist, was making a graduation speech to a sixth-grade class at PS 121. This class had a group of children with absolutely no hope of ever going to college. In fact, there was very little hope that most of these children would even graduate from high school. But at the end of the graduation speech, Lang made a stunning offer. 'For any of you who graduate from high school, I will ensure that funds are available for you to go to college,' he said.

Of the forty-eight students in that sixth-grade class that day, forty-four graduated from high school and forty-two went to college. To put that into perspective, remember that forty per cent of inner-city students never graduate from high school, let alone go to college.

That monetary offer alone wasn't enough to ensure such great success. Lang also made sure that the students got the support they needed along the way. They were monitored and counselled through their last six years of school. But that one challenging goal, clearly articulated and within the students' reach, gave them an opportunity to visualize a future they never thought was possible. And by visualizing it for themselves, they were able to make their dreams reality.

In the words of Harvey Mackay, the best-selling business author, 'A goal is a dream with a deadline.'

Howard Marguleas is the chairman of a produce company called Sun World, and he's one of California's new breed of growers. He got to be that way by setting and meeting goal after goal. For years Marguleas had watched as the agriculture business went up and down—fat times, lean times, as impossible to predict as they were to control. At least that's how everyone said the fruit-and-vegetable business worked.

But Marguleas had a goal: to develop new and unique kinds of produce that could withstand the shifts in the tides of consumer buying. 'This business is really no different from real estate,' Marguleas reasoned. 'When the market's down, unless you have something very highly, uniquely different, you're in serious trouble. Same thing in agriculture. If you're just another producer of lettuce, carrots or oranges, and you have nothing different from anyone else, you do well only if there's a short supply. If there's a large supply, you won't do well. And that's what we've tried to adjust to, to find the windows of opportunity that come with being different, a niche in the marketplace.'

That's where the idea of a better pepper came from. Yes, a better pepper. If he could develop a pepper that was tastier than the peppers that other people grew, Marguleas assured himself, wouldn't the grocers of America want to stock it in good times and in bad?

So he did it, giving birth to the Le Rouge Royal pepper. 'It's an elongated, three-lobe pepper,' Marguleas says. 'We were told, you know, "You have to have a bell pepper, a square-shaped pepper, to sell." But once we tasted this pepper—the colour, the flavour, everything about it—we knew we had something. We knew that if we promoted it properly and advertised and merchandised it and put a name on it, we could get people to eat it. And once they ate it, they were going to continue to buy it.'

What all this taught Marguleas is, 'Never cease to pursue the opportunity to seek something different. Don't be satisfied with what you're doing. Always try to seek a way and a method to improve upon what you're doing, even if it's considered contrary to the traditions of an industry.'

Those who fail to establish independent goals for themselves become, in Marguleas's word, the 'me-toos' of the world. The me-toos, the people who follow but don't lead, do fine when times are good. But when times get tough, they inevitably get left behind.

Marguleas had his finger on something there. People who set goals—challenging goals, but goals that are also achievable— are the ones with solid grips on their futures; the ones who end up accomplishing extraordinary things.

Reebok International, Ltd., the athletic-shoe company, set a major corporate goal for itself: get Shaquille O'Neal. The Orlando Magic star wasn't going to come easy. Lots of major companies were eager to hire him as their spokesman.

'It was a question of convincing him that we had the best commitment to him, that we were willing to do something to create for him a program that the next guy couldn't do,' says Paul Fireman, Reebok's chairman.

The whole company geared up. 'We created an ad campaign before he was here. We created it for him exclusively. We spent money to create it, and we really put our effort in. We were just absolutely committed to getting him. We took a gamble. We took a risk. We spent the money, the time, and the commitment.' Sometimes that's what setting goals is all about.

'It would have been a major confrontation emotionally if we had lost,' Fireman said. 'If we didn't go so far to get him here, we wouldn't have had the loss emotionally. But we wouldn't have had the player, either.'

Goals aren't important only for companies. They're the building blocks that successful careers are made of.

Jack Gallagher worked in the family tyre business, where he had held just about every job—accounting, bookkeeping, manufacturing and sales. All that experience in the tyre business taught him one thing for sure: he didn't want to work in the tyre business.

One day Gallagher ran into a high-school friend who was working as an assistant administrator at a local hospital. 'That's what I'd like to do,' Gallagher told himself. 'I'd love to help people. I'd love to have a big business, and I'd love to lead a group for the right things.' There were several giant hurdles between Jack Gallagher and a hospital administrator's job—a graduate degree in hospital administration, for one thing, and a job at a hospital, for another.

But Gallagher had his goal, and he got started jumping the hurdles right away.

He talked his way into Yale. He won a stipend from the

Kellogg Foundation. He got a loan from a local bank. He worked nights in the business office of North Shore University Hospital. And after he got the graduate degree, he applied for an administrative residency at North Shore.

'I interviewed with Jack Hausman, the chairman of the hospital's board,' Gallagher recalls. 'I must have spent three minutes with him, and I sold him in three minutes. He asked me a funny question. He knew I was married and had three kids. He said, "How are you going to afford it?" They paid thirty-nine hundred for a resident then.'

Gallagher recalls how he responded, 'Look, Mr Hausman, I thought it out a long time before I came to see you here. I had to have everything set so I could live during this residency and move into an administrative role after that.'

He had a goal. He planned every detail. He worked tirelessly toward them. He's North Shore's CEO today.

Singer-songwriter Neil Sedaka, whose pop-music career has spanned more than three decades, learned to set goals when he was just a kid. Sedaka grew up in a rough part of Brooklyn, and he was never one of the tough guys. His earliest goal was a perfectly understandable one: to be liked and thereby stay alive through high school.

'I wasn't a fighter,' Sedaka explained recently. 'So I had to be liked. I always wanted to be liked. You know how it is. You're always afraid of getting into a fight.' Anyway, young Neil came up with what turned out to be an ingenious method of achieving his personal goal—music.

'There was a sweetshop near Lincoln High School, and there was a jukebox in the back,' he recalled. 'All the tough kids, the leather-set kids, would hang out there, and they would listen to Elvis and Fats Domino. This was the beginning of rock and roll. So I wrote a rock-and-roll song, and I sang it, and then

I was like a hero with those leather-set kids. They even let me into their part of the sweetshop.'

The point here isn't whether Sedaka should have cared about acceptance from the tough kids. These things can seem awfully important in the high-school years. But he knew instinctively how to reach these other people—and how to achieve what was important to him at the time. For Sedaka, that high-school goal turned into a lifelong career, and this early success gave him the confidence to shoot for the stars in the future.

ROME WASN'T BUILT IN A DAY

Much the same process unfolded in the early life of Arthur Ashe, the late tennis champion. Almost single-handedly, Ashe broke down the colour barrier in professional tennis, a game that until he came along had been almost exclusively white. In his later years, Ashe fought a valiant battle against the AIDS virus, raising consciousness about the disease on ghetto street corners and in townhouse drawing rooms. His was a life of setting and reaching goals. For Ashe it started when he was a youngster on a tennis court. That's where he learned about achievement, one goal at a time.

'Breaking through that barrier, where you have set a goal and you achieve that goal, it sort of codifies whatever budding self-confidence you might have had,' Ashe said in an interview for this book just before his death.

That's how Ashe operated until the day he died. He'd set a goal and when he'd met that goal, he'd set another one. Why? 'The self-confidence itself, I think, transforms the individual,' he explained. 'It also spills over into other areas of life. Not only do you feel confident in whatever you are expert at, but you probably feel generally self-confident that you can do some other things as well, applying the same principles maybe to another task or to another set of goals.'

The goals must be realistic, and they must be attainable. Don't make the mistake of thinking you should, or can, accomplish everything today. Maybe you can't reach the moon this year, so plan a shorter trip. Set an interim goal.

Following that incremental approach, Ashe put himself on the big-time tennis map. 'My early coaches,' explained Ashe, 'set out definite goals which I bought into. The goals were not necessarily winning tennis tournaments. The goals were just things that we saw as difficult, that would require some hard work and some planning. And there was sort of an implied reward out there if I achieved those goals. Again, the goal wasn't necessarily winning this tournament or that tournament. And so incrementally, before I knew it, after I attained these mini goals along the way, all of a sudden, "Hey, I'm close to the big prize here."'

That's how Ashe always approached tough tennis matches. 'In a tournament, you'd want to get to the quarterfinals. Or in a match, you would want to not miss a certain number of backhand passing shots. Or maybe you'd want to improve your stamina to a point where you're not going to get tired when the weather is too hot. Those are the sorts of goals that help take your general focus off that long-range, elusive goal—the goal of being number one or winning the whole tournament.'

Most big challenges are best faced with a series of interim goals. That's a far more encouraging process—far more motivating too.

Dr James D. Watson, the director of the Cold Spring Harbor Laboratory, has been locked in a lifelong struggle to find the cure for cancer. Is that his only goal? Of course not. That would be too discouraging for anyone to bear. Watson has laid out a series of incremental goals for himself and his laboratory colleagues, goals they are meeting every year on the road to the ultimate cure.

'There are so many different cancers,' explains Watson, who won a Nobel prize for discovering the structure of DNA. 'We're going to cure some of them. Hopefully, we'll cure more of them.

'But you've got to pick interim goals,' he says. 'The goal is not to kill colon cancer tomorrow. It's to understand the disease. And there are many different steps. No one wants to be led into defeat. You get your happiness one small goal at a time.'

That's the way it works. Set little goals. Meet them. Set new, slightly larger goals. Meet them. Succeed.

Long before Lou Holtz became Notre Dame's head football coach, he wanted nothing more than to play the game himself. But when he went out for his high-school team, he weighed just 115 pounds.

Holtz knew this was far too small. Still, he desperately wanted to play, so he came up with a plan. He memorized all eleven positions on the team. That way, if any player got hurt, he was immediately prepared to rush onto the field. It gave him eleven chances instead of one.

'It's the same way in business today,' says writer Harvey Mackay. 'If you're working out here in the office, volunteer to learn the phone system. Volunteer to know what's going on in computers. If you're in sales, you want to know about computers.' That way, when opportunities appear, you'll have a much greater chance of seizing them. Set goals that make you more valuable to your team—as Lou Holtz did—or to your company.

The idea is to set goals and then strive to meet them. Sometimes you'll succeed on schedule, sometimes things will take longer to achieve than you thought, and sometimes you won't attain what you thought you would. Some things just aren't meant to be. The point is to keep planning and plugging away. You'll get there, just watch.

As Scalamandré Silks' Adriana Bitter says, 'Maybe we set our goals too high sometimes and we don't always reach the top end, but we certainly can start climbing that ladder.'

Without specific goals it's far too easy just to drift, never really taking charge of your life. Time gets wasted because nothing has a sense of urgency. There's no deadline. Nothing has to be done *today*. It's possible to put off anything indefinitely. Goals are what can give us direction and keep us focused.

David Luther of Corning is acutely aware of this modern propensity toward aimlessness. He worries about how it might affect his own children at home. So he's constantly talking to them about goals.

'Sometimes,' he reminds them, 'we get caught up in things.' Easy to say, of course, but how to avoid this pitfall? 'The point,' according to Luther, 'is to know yourself. Think what it is that you know and want to do. Forget the money, for a moment anyway. When you get to be the age of your parents, what is it you want to be able to point to that met your expectation, that made a difference?'

How are intelligent goals created? Mostly they just take a little thought, but there are some useful techniques for getting the mind focused on the task. You might try asking yourself the same questions Luther urges his children to ask. 'Stand back and say, "What is it I really want to be? What kind of life do I really want to lead? Am I heading in the right direction now?"' That advice makes sense no matter how far along you are in your career.

Once you establish what your goals are, prioritize them. Not everything can be done at once, so you've got to ask yourself: which comes first? What goal is most important to me now? Then try organizing your time and energy to reflect those priorities. This, often, is the most challenging part.

To prioritize his goals, Ted Owen, publisher of the *San Diego Business Journal*, follows the advice he got from a psychologist friend. 'He told me to take a piece of paper and draw a line down the centre. On the left, put any number you want. I put ten. Put the top ten things that you want to accomplish in your life before you retire at whatever age that is, one hundred or sixty or fifty.

'Put down those ten things. So you want to have a good retirement program. You want to have a nice home. You want to have a happy marriage. You want to have good health. Whatever those ten are. Then over here on the other side, you take those ten and prioritize them. One of those ten becomes number one, and so on.'

Simplistic? Maybe. But helpful too. Through this process, Owen discovered some things about himself he never knew. 'I found out that a job, a well-paying, steady job, a job that makes me feel good, was about number seven.' Once you identify your own number one, two, three' and seven, creating well-crafted goals becomes a whole lot easier.

It's fine if, over the years, those goals develop and change. 'Before I was married, I would come in on the weekends just to read the newspaper here,' says Dr Ronald Evans, a research professor at the Salk Institute for Biological Studies. 'I had nothing else to do. I loved being in labs. It was sort of a home away from home. Research is addicting,' he observes. 'It's incredibly challenging and pushes your intellectual limits. You make discoveries, and there's nothing like it.'

But life changes, pressures change and goals should be evaluated too. 'With a family now,' Evans goes on, 'it's been very difficult to change my habits, but I have. You just have to say you can't do everything.'

Corporations need goals as much as individuals do, and the same basic rules apply when companies begin defining theirs: make them clear, keep them basic and don't set too many at once.

The huge Motorola corporation was run in one recent year with just three specific goals, expressed in precise, mathematical terms: to 'continue 10-X improvement' every two years, to 'get the voice of' the customer, to 'cut business-process cycle time by factor 10' in five years.

Don't worry about what this language means. It may or may not apply at your company. What's important here is that the company has its goals. These goals are clearly understood within the company. The goals are challenging but attainable. Progress is easily measurable. And if these goals are achieved, the company will have done extraordinarily well.

Those three specific goals provide enough vision to run an entire company. Imagine what three equally clear, equally realistic goals can do for one person's life.

POINTS TO REMEMBER

1. Set a goal and never lose sight of it.
2. Your goal should be realistic and achievable.
3. Surround yourself with people who will help you reach your goals.

4

FOCUS AND DISCIPLINE

Margaret Thatcher led Britain through some of the most difficult years in the empire's history—a time that included the Falklands War, a worldwide recession and enough social upheaval to fill a century or two. Those years wrecked any number of promising political careers, and as the prime minister of Britain (not to mention the first woman ever to hold that job), Thatcher took more than her share of the heat. Yet there was one thing people on all sides of British politics had to admit: the Iron Lady never melted once. How did she manage such strength under pressure?

'If you lead a country like Britain,' Thatcher explained shortly after stepping down, 'a strong country, a country that has taken a lead in world affairs in good times and in bad, a country that is always reliable, then you have to have a touch of iron about you.'

It's really not so complicated, the former prime minister said. Stay focused. Be self-disciplined. Want desperately to succeed. 'I do not know anyone who has got to the top without hard work,' she went on. 'That is the recipe. It will not always get you to the top, but it should get you pretty near.'

Maggie Thatcher understood. Have a goal clearly in mind, something you really want; believe in yourself and be persistent;

and don't allow yourself to be distracted. In business, in family life, in sports, in politics, follow these simple rules, and your chances of succeeding are astronomically high.

THE UNFATHOMABLE DRIVE

Ivan Stewart was a man with a goal. He had a life-long dream of competing in long-distance off-road auto racing—races of three hundred, five hundred, one thousand miles across rugged terrain, involving hours and hours of intense concentration and intense backaches. But Stewart was a general superintendent in the construction business with a wife, a mortgage and three growing kids. He had responsibilities. He had commitments. The odds were way against his reaching his goal, but he also had a plan and lots of energy to pursue it.

'I wanted to be involved in racing, so I worked on the race cars after work and on Saturday and Sunday. Then I got a chance to ride, just to be involved, never thinking at the time—not at all—that it would ever get professional,' Stewart says.

One day his opportunity arrived. A driver Stewart had been working with broke his leg just before a race. The car was ready and entered. He had no choice but to let Stewart drive.

So with his friend Earl Stahl sitting in the passenger seat, Stewart set out in the race. Everything went to hell. They ran into an embankment. The car flipped over. They got stuck in the mud. The other cars were whizzing by. His one chance of proving himself looked irretrievably lost.

'By now we're the last car,' he says, recalling that very first race. 'Everybody's gone. They start one car every thirty seconds, and there were probably sixty cars, seventy cars in that race. Everybody's gone. Here's Earl and I, now we're last. We didn't go another ten miles, fifteen miles, twenty miles, whatever it was, when the throttle—this is a Volkswagen-powered car—the cable that goes from your foot back to the carburettor broke. So now I can't even drive. I said, "Earl, get a crescent wrench." Earl gets the crescent wrench out of the tool box, and I pull out the wire that's broken, and it's just long enough to pull around the crescent wrench so I can wrap it around the crescent. We do this pretty quick. Within five or ten minutes we've got a hand throttle going so I can push the throttle and I can push the clutch and I can drive one-handed. No power steering though. This is determination—and I want to drive.

'I said to Earl, "I need you to shift it," because it's a four-speed transmission. "I'm going to give you an elbow every time I want to change." So I'd push the throttle, and we were so messed up, I'd have the clutch in, the throttle on and he'd be in the wrong gear. Anyway, we got going pretty good. I'd give the throttle and lay off the throttle. I'd push the clutch in and give him an elbow and he'd give me a higher gear. Pretty soon he realized what we wanted to do. We were messed up because once in a while he'd give me a low gear and I wanted a high gear and vice versa. But we got pretty good at it. Pretty soon we started catching—this is a three-hundred-mile race. We catch one, we catch another one. Teamwork. Yes, we got good at it. Pretty soon we were really driving. You know, we were driving, and to make a long story short, we won that race. Won that three-hundred-mile race.' That kind of focus and self-discipline is what it takes to win the race in all parts of life.

Stewart went on to become the top off-road driver in America. He's won the prestigious Valvoline oil Iron Man trophy—the sport's Heismann and Super Bowl rolled into one—so many times that his fans now know him simply as Iron Man. And at forty-seven years old—ancient in this body-jarring sport—Stewart signed another three-year sponsorship deal with Toyota.

'They know I'm getting older, and there's a lot of young kids coming in.' But that's just another challenge, not a reason to give up. Who knows? Iron Man will probably still be racing at sixty. It's that kind of focus—whatever the field of endeavour—that separates the achievers from the nonachievers.

'That's the single biggest secret to raising major money,' says Thomas A. Saunders III at Saunders Karp & Company.

'When I was raising this big fund a few years ago for Morgan Stanley,' Saunders recalls, 'we had an assignment to go in and raise for our merchant banking business two hundred million dollars. We raised two-point-three billion. It was the second-largest amount of money that's ever been assembled for a pure equity fund. I think an awful lot of the success of that was just stick-to-itiveness, not being prepared to go in and be turned off. Not being prepared to accept no for an answer, a willingness to come back at it again. A willingness to keep pushing. A willingness to find out why someone said no—and maybe convince the person to say yes.'

Fred Sievert is chief financial officer at New York Life Insurance Company. The person he learned his perseverance from was his father, whose name is also Fred. 'The one love in his life was playing the trumpet,' Sievert says of his father. 'He played with some of the best big bands, including Harry James, Artie Shaw and Jack Teagarden. He's a very exceptional trumpet player.'

And even the father never stopped practicing the basics. 'He would play scales,' the son says. 'Here's a guy who's already one of the best trumpet players in the country, and what's he doing? He's not playing some lengthy new tune that he wants to learn. He's playing the scales. Hour after hour, day after day. He would play these different scales. He would say to me that if he knew the scales and he could play them quickly, he could learn any song there was.'

That same unshakable focus is what propelled two Southern governors, sixteen years apart, all the way to the White House. One was a soft-spoken peanut farmer from Georgia by the name of Jimmy Carter. The other came from a little dot on the map called Hope, Arkansas. His name is Bill Clinton.

When Carter started his 1976 campaign, few of the big-time national political pros gave him much of a chance. Hardly anyone outside Georgia had ever heard of him, he was facing a crowded field of higher-profile Democrats, and the campaign's first major hurdle was New Hampshire, about as far from home as this Georgian could get.

When Clinton ran in 1992, he was thought to face similarly long odds—and the reasons were mostly the same. He was a little better known than Carter had been, but not much so, and the sitting Republican president had just won a hugely popular war.

If you believed the early experts, neither one of these governors had much of a chance. By the end of the early primaries, these two sons of Dixie were supposed to be out of the running. That's not what happened, of course, and there are many reasons why. None of them was more important than the focus and the discipline of these two campaigns.

In the course of these gruelling races, both men had many reasons to give up. For Carter, besides his utter obscurity, there was the threat of Ted Kennedy and the nagging perception that Kennedy, not Carter, was the choice of 'real Democrats'. For Clinton, there were the claims of Gennifer Flowers, the count-him-out editorials, the power of a sitting president, and a fellow named Perot.

Those odds didn't stop Carter in 1976. They didn't stop Clinton in 1992. And the biggest reason both times was that both men were focused. They knew exactly what they wanted to achieve. They were working toward a specific goal, a dream each man had held since childhood. As a result, they had superhuman motivation. They worked like crazy, kept their eyes on the ball and they won the prize.

Persistence is the other part of the equation. To get what you want in life, you've got to believe in yourself and you've got to be willing to keep after it. Try again and again and again.

CONSISTENCY IS CHIEF

Burt Manning of J. Walter Thompson, one of the world's largest advertising agencies, started in the business as a copywriter. He became the only 'creative person' ever to head the company, which has produced campaigns for such major clients as Ford, Lever Brothers, Nestlé, Kellogg, Kodak, Goodyear and Warner-Lambert.

Yes, talent and creativity are vital in a business as competitive as advertising, but without hard, well-focused and persistent work, all that talent and creativity can come to naught. It's a lesson Manning learned first-hand, early in his career.

He came up with what he thought was a great campaign for his first big client. The client was Schlitz and the slogan Manning was urging was one that would become as famous as 'Mmm-mmm good': *'When you're out of Schlitz, you're out of beer.'* Manning was high on the campaign, but hard as this is to believe today, the Schlitz Brewing Company was not. The Schlitz people considered the whole idea too negative. They wanted Manning to come up with something more upbeat.

Manning wasn't about to give up. He went back to the customer again and again, presenting the campaign a total of six times. He recalls the final reaction, 'I was able to bring it back so many times essentially because I had a relationship with this client that permitted me to and didn't make him throw me out of the room. On the sixth time he said, "All right. I don't really think this is right, but if you guys do, test it somewhere."

The rest, of course is advertising history. Manning's talent and creativity dreamed up a first-rate campaign, but only his hard work and persistence delivered it to the public. Patience and perseverance will accomplish more in this world than a brilliant dash. Remember that when something goes wrong.

Don't let anything discourage you. Keep on. Never give up. That had been the policy of most of those who have succeeded. Of course, discouragement will come. The important thing is to surmount it. If you can do that, the world is yours.

What this means, in practical terms, is that you've got to remember what the basic goal is—whether it's selling an ad campaign, winning an auto race or getting elected to the presidency of the United States. Then work single-mindedly toward that goal.

And be sure to follow through. That's not always easy. You have to train yourself to march through every step, to complete every detail of every job every time. That's what makes people more valuable to a company, more crucial to an organization, more trustworthy to their colleagues and friends—following through on every detail.

'When I walk into an office and I see a stack of return calls to be made—you know, a big stack—I think to myself, "This guy's out of control,"' says E. Martin Gibson, chief executive officer of Corning Lab Services, Inc. 'That raises a little question about your dependability, if you don't even return your calls. It's little things.'

People who prove themselves dependable are given greater opportunities to show how dependable they can really be. 'People know they can depend on you,' Gibson says. 'They ask you to do something, and they don't make a follow-up note.

They know you'll do it. That's dependability. Don't be one of these flaky characters who doesn't return phone calls, who gets a memo from the chairman and doesn't know quite how to answer it and sticks it aside and forgets about it. The chairman's up there wondering, "What is wrong with this bozo?"'

It is in those disciplined details—hundreds and thousands of little details—that success or failure is found every day. 'It's old values, like getting to an appointment early, remembering to follow through on your promises and having pride in your work,' says Joyce Harvey of Harmon Associates Corporation. 'If you're doing a letter of credit, you've got to follow steps one to four. You can't skip step three. Mistakes are costly. Don't move too fast. Check your details, and stay focused.'

ATTITUDE GOES A LONG WAY

Ross Greenburg discovered the importance of discipline and concentration that night in 1990 when Mike Tyson was knocked out by Buster Douglas. Tyson was at that point the undisputed heavyweight champion of the world. Douglas was a tough fighter, but up to the opening bell, he wasn't given much of a shot.

Greenburg is executive producer of HBO Sports. By the time of the Tyson-Douglas match, he had already produced more than one hundred title fights for television. But even for a veteran like Greenburg, concentration can sometimes be shaken by dramatic events.

As Greenburg recalls, 'In about the second round, it was obvious that something was right with Douglas and very wrong with Tyson. Tyson had eaten three or four straight jabs and my announcers and I immediately pounced on the story line.' So far, so good.

'In the fourth round, Douglas threw a combination

that rocked Tyson, and there was a loud scream on our communication line. Everyone in our truck started realizing what we were seeing in front of us. For one of the very rare times, we were getting caught up in the sporting event rather than in our individual jobs. I can remember it vividly, and all the people that work with me will tell you the same story. When I sensed this, I said, "Okay, everybody relax. Let's remember we have a job to do here. If you let yourself become too tied to the event, you'll lose sight of the work at hand." That's all it took. Immediately everybody was cut off from that basic, visceral reaction to the event, and we worked our way back into the job—providing replays of the staggering combinations.'

There just isn't much room for slipups on live TV. 'See, if I get caught up in rooting for Douglas at that point, I won't be able to cue up my tape machines and my ads. My associate directors won't be able to cue those points so you will see that replay when the round is over, which is our job.'

But Greenburg admits that even he came close to losing his focus on that memorable night. 'I will never, ever forget—I will never, ever forget—the moment that Tyson hit the canvas. It was as if I were reading some historical account of heavyweight championship boxing and at that split second, I saw the page turn and I was going to the new chapter and the new heavyweight champion. I'll take that to my grave. Tyson-Douglas, and maybe there will be another event down the line. I'll just be able to say, "I was part of that."'

Steely focus isn't important just in sports television. In the case of Dr Scott Coyne, this same kind of focus and discipline literally made the difference between life and death.

Coyne, a radiologist who had once studied for the priesthood, was the first doctor on the scene when an Avianca Boeing 727 crashed near his home on Long Island one wretched

January night. For more than an hour Coyne was the only doctor on the scene.

One by one he had to tend to the passengers' injuries. He also had to soothe their nerves. He had to do it all in just a minute or two with each person on the ground, and he had to do it without language, since most of the people on the plane were from Colombia and didn't speak any English. Coyne's Spanish didn't go much beyond '*Doc-tor, doc-tor.*' He made himself understood by focussing every fibre of his being, Coyne said. He found a way to make this work.

'I had a stethoscope on,' he says, remembering that crazy night. 'I kept saying, "*Doc-tor*," and some of them were crying and screaming. You don't know if they're screaming because they're scared or because they're broken apart. I was able to communicate by touching the faces. You could tell how bad they'd been hurt by how they looked at you.

'I had to whisper in their ears. I had to maintain my composure and hold them and try to reassure them just by my expression and by my touch and holding their faces. I was unable to get a history from anybody. You know, you can't ask them where they're hurting: how bad does it hurt? Does the back hurt? I had to literally check every patient from head to toe, and then as I went down the row, I'd find these fractures were just grotesque. I'd never seen fractures like this. Legs were literally hanging off. And you check these fractures and start IVs the best you can, and you go to the next patient and start all over and check the rib cage—by hand. They couldn't tell you. You couldn't even say, "Point," so they could understand what you're saying. Well, it was a surreal experience because when you're going through it, the adrenaline is so high.'

Focus. Intense one hundred per cent focus. That's what got Coyne through.

Coyne's focus was so intense that everything peripheral was just blocked out of his mind. He discovered just how focused he had been later when he spoke about the accident at a stress-management seminar. The others in the group were describing all the mayhem you'd expect in that kind of circumstance: ambulances and fire trucks and squawking radios and screaming survivors and rescue workers yelling back and forth. Coyne heard none of it.

'What I remember is how quiet it was. It all seemed so quiet and orderly. I didn't hear anything. You had to focus so much you didn't hear. It was like a trance. All I remember is just walking in utter silence. I never heard a thing. The only thing I did hear was helicopters about an hour later. Helicopters came in to evacuate some of the injured people.'

Focus, the ability to ignore distractions and pursue only what is important—that's what made the difference that night and helped save all those lives.

POINTS TO REMEMBER

1. Constant hard work guarantees success.
2. Be focused and disciplined towards your goal.
3. Never give up.

5

INCREASE COURAGE AND SELF-CONFIDENCE

More than eighteen thousand businesspersons, since 1912, have been members of the various public speaking courses conducted by me. Most of them have, at my request, written stating why they had enrolled for this training and what they hoped to obtain from it. Naturally, the phraseology varied; but the central desire in these letters, the basic want in the vast majority, remained surprisingly the same, 'When I am called upon to stand up and speak,' man after man wrote, 'I become so self-conscious, so frightened, that I can't think clearly, can't concentrate, can't remember what I had intended to say. I want to gain self-confidence, poise and the ability to think on my feet. I want to get my thoughts together in logical order and I want to be able to say my say clearly and convincingly before a business group or audience.' Thousands of their confessions sounded about like that. Years ago, a gentleman here called D.W. Ghent joined my public speaking course in Philadelphia. Shortly after the opening session, he invited me to lunch with him in the Manufacturers' Club. He was a man of middle age and had always led an active life; was head of his own manufacturing establishment, a leader in church work and civic activities. While we were having lunch that day, he leaned across the table and said, 'I have been asked many times to talk before various gatherings but I have never been able to do so. I get so fussed, my mind becomes an utter blank: so I have sidestepped it all my life. But I am chairman now of a board of college trustees. I must preside at their meetings. Do you think it will be possible for me to learn to speak at this late date in my life?'

'Do I *think*, Mr Ghent?' I replied. 'It is *not* a question of my *thinking*. I *know you can*, and I *know you will* if you will only practise and follow the directions and instructions.'

After he had completed his training, we lost touch with each other for a while. In 1921, we met and lunched together again at the Manufacturers' Club. We sat in the same corner and occupied the same table that we had had on the first occasion. Reminding him of our former conversation, I asked him if I had been too sanguine then. He took a little red-backed notebook out of his pocket and showed me a list of talks and dates for which he was booked. 'And the ability to make these,' he confessed, 'the pleasure I get in doing it, the additional service I can render to the community—these are among the most gratifying things in my life.'

The International Conference for the Limitation of Armaments had been held in Washington shortly before that. When it was known that Lloyd George was planning to attend it, the Baptists of Philadelphia cabled, inviting him to speak at a great mass meeting to be held in their city. Lloyd George cabled back that if he came to Washington, he would accept their invitation. And Mr Ghent informed me that he himself had been chosen, from among all the Baptists of that city, to introduce England's premier to the audience.

And this was the man who had sat at that same table less than three years before and solemnly asked me if I thought he would ever be able to talk in public!

Was the rapidity with which he forged ahead in his speaking ability unusual? Not at all. There have been hundreds of similar cases. For example—to quote one more specific instance—years ago, a Brooklyn physician, whom we will call Dr Curtis, spent the winter in Florida near the training grounds of the Giants. Being an enthusiastic baseball fan, he often went to see them practise. In time, he became quite friendly with the team and was invited to attend a banquet given in their honour.

After the coffee and nuts were served, several prominent guests were called upon to 'say a few words'. Suddenly, with the abruptness and unexpectedness of an explosion, he heard the toast-master remark, 'We have a physician with us tonight, and I am going to ask Dr Curtis to talk on a baseball player's health.'

Was he prepared? Of course. He had had the best preparation in the world: he had been studying hygiene and practising medicine for almost a third of a century. He could have sat in his chair and talked about this subject all night to the man seated on his right or left. But to get up and say the same things to even a small audience—that was another matter. That was a paralysing matter. His heart doubled its pace and skipped beats at the very contemplation of it. He had never made a public speech in his life, and every thought that he had had now took wings.

What was he to do? The audience was applauding. Everyone was looking at him. He shook his head. But that served only to heighten the applause, to increase the demand. The cries of 'Dr Curtis! Speech! Speech!' grew louder and more insistent.

He was in positive misery. He knew that if he got up, he would fail, that he would be unable to utter half a dozen sentences. So he arose and, without saying a word, turned his back on his friends and walked silently out of the room, a deeply embarrassed and humiliated man.

Small wonder that one of the first things he did after getting back to Brooklyn was to come to the Central Y.M.C.A. and enrol in the course in public speaking. He didn't propose to be put to the blush and be stricken dumb a second time.

He was the kind of student that delights an instructor: he was in dead earnest. He wanted to be able to talk, and there was no half-heartedness about his desires. He prepared his talks thoroughly, he practised them with a will and he never missed a single session of the course.

He did precisely what such a student always does: he progressed at a rate that surprised him, that surpassed his fondest hopes. After the first few sessions his nervousness subsided, and his confidence mounted higher and higher. In two months, he had become the star speaker of the group. He was soon accepting invitations to speak elsewhere; he now loved the feel and exhilaration of it, the distinction and the additional friends it brought him.

PRACTICE MAKES A MAN PERFECT

The gaining of self-confidence and courage and the ability to think calmly and clearly while talking to a group is not one-tenth as difficult as most men imagine. It is not a gift bestowed by Providence on only a few rarely endowed individuals. It is like the ability to play golf. Any man can develop his own latent capacity if he has sufficient desire to do so.

Is there the faintest shadow of a reason why you should not be able to think as well in a perpendicular position before an audience as you can when sitting down? Surely, you know there is not. In fact, you ought to think better when facing a group of men. Their presence ought to stir you and lift you. A great many speakers will tell you that the presence of an audience is a stimulus, an inspiration, that drives their brains to function more clearly, more keenly. At such times, thoughts, facts, ideas, that they did not know they possessed, drift smoking by, as Henry Ward Beecher said; and they have but to reach out and lay their hands hot upon them. They ought to be your experience. It probably will be if you practise and persevere.

Of this much, however, you may be absolutely sure: training and practise will wear away your audience-fright and give you self-confidence and an abiding courage.

Do not imagine that your case is unusually difficult. Even those who afterwards became the most eloquent representatives of their generation were, at the outset of their careers, afflicted by this blinding fear and self-consciousness.

Mark Twain, the first time he stood up to lecture, felt as if his mouth were filled with cotton and his pulse were speeding for some prize cup.

The late Jean Jaurès, the most powerful political speaker that France produced during his generation, sat, for a year, tongue-tied in the Chamber of Deputies before he could summon up the courage to make his initial speech.

John Bright, the illustrious Englishman who, during the civil war, defended in England the cause of union and emancipation, made his maiden speech before a group of countryfolk gathered in a school building. He was so frightened on the way to the place, so fearful that he would fail, that he implored his companion to start applause to bolster him up whenever he showed signs of giving way to his nervousness.

Charles Stewart Parnell, the great Irish leader, at the outset of his speaking career, was so nervous, according to the testimony of his brother, that he frequently clenched his fists until his nails sank into his flesh and his palms bled.

Disraeli admitted that he would rather have led a cavalry charge than have faced the House of Commons for the first time. His opening speech there was a ghastly failure. So was Sheridan's.

In fact, so many of the famous speakers of England have made poor showings at first that there is now a feeling in Parliament that it is rather an inauspicious omen for a young man's initial talk to be a decided success. So take heart.

After watching the careers and aiding somewhat in the development of so many speakers, the author is always glad when a student has, at the outset, a certain amount of flutter and nervous agitation.

There is a certain responsibility in making a talk, even if it is to only two dozen men in a business conference—a certain strain, a certain shock, a certain excitement. The speaker ought to be keyed up like a thoroughbred straining at the bit. The immortal Cicero said, two thousand years ago, that all public speaking of real merit was characterized by nervousness.

Speakers often experience this same feeling even when they are talking over the radio. 'Microphone fright', it is called. When Charlie Chaplin went 'on the air', he had his speech all written out. Surely he was used to audiences. He toured America back in 1912 with a vaudeville sketch entitled 'A Night in a Music Hall'. Before that he was on the legitimate stage in England. Yet, when he went into the padded room and faced the microphone, he had a feeling in the stomach not unlike the sensation one gets when he crosses the Atlantic during a stormy February.

James Kirkwood, a famous motion picture actor and director, had a similar experience. He used to be a star on the speaking stage; but when he came out of the sending room after addressing the invisible audience, he was mopping perspiration from his brow. 'An opening night on Broadway,' he confessed, 'is nothing in comparison to that.'

Some men, no matter how often they speak, always experience this self-consciousness just before they commence; but in a few seconds after they have got on their feet, it disappears.

Even Lincoln felt shy for the few opening moments. In a few moments he gained composure and warmth and earnestness, and his real speech began.

Your experience may be similar to his.

THE PRE-REQUISITES

In order to get the most out of this training, and to get it with rapidity and dispatch, four things are essential:

FIRST
Start With a Strong and Persistent Desire

This is of far more importance than you probably realize. If your instructor could look into your mind and heart now and ascertain the depth of your desires, he could foretell, almost with certainty, the swiftness of the progress you will make. If your desire is pale and flabby, your achievements will also take on that hue and consistency. But, if you go after this subject with persistence, and with the energy of a bulldog after a cat, nothing underneath the Milky Way will defeat you.

Therefore, arouse your enthusiasm for this study. Enumerate its benefits. Think of what additional self-confidence and the ability to talk more convincingly in business will mean to you. Think of what it may mean to you socially; of the friends it will bring, of the increase of your personal influence, of the leadership it will give you. And it will give you leadership more rapidly than almost any other activity you can think of or imagine.

It is an attainment that almost every person of education longs for. After Andrew Carnegie's death there was found, among his papers, a plan for his life drawn up when he was thirty-three years of age. He then felt that in two more years he could so arrange his business as to have an annual income of fifty thousand dollars; so he proposed to retire at thirty-five, go to Oxford and get a thorough education, and *pay special attention to speaking in public.*

Think of the glow of satisfaction and pleasure that will accrue from the exercise of this new power. The author has travelled round over no small part of this terrestrial ball; and has had many and varied experiences; but for downright, and lasting inward satisfaction, he knows of few things that will compare to standing before an audience and making men think your thoughts after you. It will give you a sense of strength, a feeling of power. It will appeal to your pride of personal accomplishment. It will set you off from and raise you above your fellowmen. There is magic in it and a never-to-be-forgotten thrill. 'Two minutes before I begin,' a speaker confessed, 'I would rather be whipped than start; but two minutes before I finish, I would rather be shot than stop.'

In every course, some men grow faint-hearted and fall by the wayside; so you should keep thinking of what this course will mean to you until your desire is white hot. You should start this programme with an enthusiasm that will carry you through every session, triumphant to the end. Tell your friends that you have joined this course. Set aside one certain night of the week for the reading of these lessons and the preparation of your talks. In short, make it as easy as possible to go ahead. Make it as difficult as possible to retreat.

When Julius Caesar sailed over the channel from Gaul and landed with his legions on what is now England, what did he do to ensure the success of his arms? A very clever thing: he halted his soldiers on the chalk cliffs of Dover, and, looking down over the waves two hundred feet below, they saw red tongues of fire consume every ship in which they had crossed. In the enemy's country, with the last link with the Continent gone, the last means of retreating burned, there was but one thing left for them to do: to advance, to conquer. That is precisely what they did.

Such was the spirit of the immortal Caesar. Why not make it yours, too, in this war to exterminate your foolish fear of audiences.

SECOND
Act Confidently

To develop courage when you are facing an audience, act as if you already have it. Of course, unless you are prepared, all the acting in the world will avail but little. But granted that you know what you are going to talk about, step out briskly and take a deep breath. In fact, breathe deeply for thirty seconds before you ever face your audience. The increased supply of oxygen will buoy you up and give you courage. The great tenor, Jean de Reszke, used to say that when you had your breath so you 'could sit on it', nervousness vanished.

When a youth of the Peuhl tribe in Central Africa attains manhood and wishes to take unto himself a wife, he is compelled to undergo the ceremony of flagellation. The women of the tribe foregather, singing and clapping their hands to the rhythm of tom-toms. The candidate strides forth stripped naked to the waist. Suddenly a man armed with a cruel whip sets upon the lad, beating his bare skin, lashing him, flogging him like a fiend. Welts appear; often the skin is cut, blood flows; scars are made that last a lifetime. During this scourging, a venerable judge of the tribe crouches at the feet of the victim to see if he moves or exhibits the slightest evidence of pain. To pass the test successfully the tortured aspirant must not only endure the ordeal, but, as he endures it, he must sing a paean of praise.

In every age, in every clime, men have always admired courage; so, no matter how your heart may be pounding inside, stride forth bravely, stop, stand still like the scourged youth of Central Africa, and like him, act as if you loved it.

Draw yourself up to your full height, look your audience straight in the eyes and begin to talk as confidently as if every one of them owed you money. Imagine that they do. Imagine that they have assembled there to bet you for an extension of credit. The psychological effect on you will be beneficial.

Do not nervously button and unbutton your coat, and fumble with your hands. If you must make nervous movements, place your hands behind your back and twist your fingers there where no one can see the performance—or wiggle your toes.

As a general rule, it is bad for a speaker to hide behind furniture, but it may give you a little courage the first few times to stand behind a table or chair and to grip them tightly—or hold a coin firmly in the palm of your hand.

How did Theodore Roosevelt develop his characteristic courage and self-reliance? Was he endowed by nature with a venturesome and daring spirit? Not at all. 'Having been a rather sickly and awkward boy,' he confesses in his *Autobiography*, 'I was, as a young man, at first both nervous and distrustful of my own prowess. I had to train myself painfully and laboriously not merely as regards my body but as regards my soul and spirit.'

Fortunately, he has told us how he achieved the transformation, 'When a boy,' he writes, 'I read a passage in one of Marryat's books which always impressed me. In this passage the captain of some small British man-of-war is explaining to the hero how to acquire the quality of fearlessness. He says that at the outset almost every man is frightened when he goes into action, but that the course to follow is for the man to keep such a grip on himself that he can act just as if he were not frightened. After this is kept up long enough, it changes from pretence to reality, and the man does in very fact become fearless by sheer dint of practising fearlessness when he does not feel it. (I am using my own language, not Marryat's.)

'This was the theory upon which I went. There were all kinds of things of which I was afraid at first, ranging from grizzly bears to "mean" horses and gun-fighters; but by acting as if I was not afraid I gradually ceased to be afraid. Most men can have the same experience if they choose.'

So take the offensive against your fears. Go out to meet them, battle them, conquer them by sheer boldness at every opportunity.

Have a message, and then think of yourself as a courier boy instructed to deliver it. We pay slight attention to the boy. It is the courier that we want. The message—that is the thing. Keep your mind on it. Keep your heart in it. Know it like the back of your hand. Believe it feelingly. Then talk as if you were determined to say it. Do that, and the chances are ten to one that you will soon be master of the occasion and master of yourself.

THIRD
Know Thoroughly What You Are Going to Talk About

Unless a man has thought out and planned his talk and knows what he is going to say, he can't feel very comfortable when he faces his auditors. He is like the blind leading the blind. Under such circumstances, your speaker ought to be self-conscious, ought to feel repentant, ought to be ashamed of his negligence.

'I was elected to the Legislature in the autumn of 1881,' Theodore Roosevelt wrote in his *Autobiography*, 'and found myself the youngest man in that body. Like all young men and inexperienced members, I had considerable difficulty in teaching myself to speak. I profited much by the advice of a hard-headed old countryman—who was unconsciously paraphrasing the Duke of Wellington, who was himself doubtless paraphrasing somebody else. The advice ran, "Don't speak until you are sure you have something to say, and know just what it is; then say it, and sit down."'

This 'hard-headed old countryman' ought to have told Roosevelt of another aid in overcoming nervousness. He ought to have added, 'It will help you to throw off your embarrassment if you can find something to do before an audience—if you can exhibit something, write a word on the blackboard or point out a spot on the map, or move a table or throw open a window, or shift some books and papers—any physical action with a purpose behind it may help you to feel more at home.'

True, it is not always easy to find an excuse for doing such things, but there is the suggestion. Use it if you can, but use it the first few times only. A baby does not cling to chairs after it learns to walk.

FOURTH
Practise! Practise! Practise!

The last point we have to make here is emphatically the most important. Even though you forget everything you have read so far, do remember this: the first way, the last way, the never-failing way to develop self-confidence in speaking is—to speak. Really the whole matter finally simmers down to but one essential: practise, practise, practise. That is the *sine qua non* of it all, 'the without which not'.

'Any beginner,' warned Roosevelt, 'is apt to have "buck fever". "Buck fever" means a state of intense nervous excitement which may be entirely divorced from timidity. It may affect a man the first time he has to speak to a large audience just as it may affect him the first time he sees a buck-deer or goes into battle. What such a man needs is not courage, but nerve control and cool-headedness. This he can get only by actual practice. He must, by custom and repeated exercise of self-mastery, get his nerves thoroughly under control. This is largely a matter of habit; in the sense of repeated effort and repeated exercise of willpower. If the man has the right stuff in him, he will grow stronger and stronger with each exercise of it.'

So, persevere. Don't remain away from any session of the course because the business duties of the week have rendered it impossible for you to prepare something. Prepared or unprepared, come. Let the instructor, the class, suggest a topic for you after you have come before them.

You want to get rid of your audience fear? Let us see what causes it.

Fear is the result of a lack of confidence and what causes that? It is the result of not knowing what you can really do. And not knowing what you can do is caused by a lack of experience.

When you get a record of successful experience behind you, your fears will vanish; they will melt like night mists under the glare of a July sun.

One thing is certain: the accepted way to learn to swim is to plunge into the water. You have been reading this book long enough. Let us toss it aside now, and get busy with the real work in hand.

Choose your subject, preferably one on which you have some knowledge, and construct a three-minute talk. Practise the talk by yourself a number of times. Then give it, if possible, to the group for whom it is intended, or before your class, putting into the effort all your force and power.

POINTS TO REMEMBER

1. The only way to win over fear of public speaking is by training and practicing.
2. Importance of body language to appear confident.
3. Believe in the subject of your speech if you want the audience to believe it.

6

ACQUIRING THE BASIC SKILLS

I started teaching classes in public speaking in 1912, the year the Titanic went down in the icy waters of the North Atlantic.

Over the years, at these classes, people are given the opportunity of sharing what they hope to gain from this training. Naturally, the phraseology varies; but the central desire, the basic want in the vast majority of cases, remains surprisingly the same, 'When I am called upon to stand up and speak, I become so self-conscious, so frightened, that I can't think clearly, can't concentrate, can't remember what I intended to say. I want to gain self-confidence, poise and the ability to think on my feet. I want to get my thoughts together in logical order, and I want to be able to talk clearly and convincingly before a business or social group.'

Does this sound familiar? Have you experienced these same feelings of inadequacy? Would you give a small fortune to have the ability to speak convincingly and persuasively in public? The very fact that you have begun reading this book is proof of your interest in acquiring the ability to speak effectively.

I know what you are going to say, what you would say if you could talk to me, 'But Mr Carnegie, do you really think I could develop the confidence to get up and face a group of people and address them in a coherent, fluent manner?'

I have spent nearly all my life helping people get rid of their fears and develop courage and confidence. I could fill many books with the stories of the miracles that have taken place in my classes. It is not, therefore, a question of my *thinking*. I *know* you can, if you practice the directions and suggestions that you will find in this book.

Is there the faintest shadow of a reason why you should not be able to think as well in a perpendicular position before an audience as you can sitting down? Is there any reason why you should play host to butterflies in your stomach and become a victim of the 'trembles' when you get up to address an audience? Surely, you realize that this condition can be remedied, that training and practice will wear away your audience-fright and give you self-confidence.

This book will help you to achieve that goal. It is not an ordinary textbook. It is not filled with rules concerning the mechanics of speaking. It does not dwell on the physiological aspects of vocal production and articulation. It is the distillation of a lifetime spent in training adults in effective speaking. It starts with you as you are, and from that premise works naturally to the conclusion of what you want to be. All you have to do is cooperate—follow the suggestions in this book, apply them in every speaking situation and persevere.

In order to get the most out of this book, and to get it with rapidity and dispatch, you will find these four guideposts useful:

FIRST
Take Heart from Others' Experience

There is no such animal, in or out of captivity, as a born public speaker. In those periods of history when public speaking was a refined art that demanded close attention to the laws of rhetoric and the niceties of delivery, it was even more difficult to be born a public speaker. Now we think of public speaking as a kind of enlarged conversation. Gone forever is the old grandiloquent style and the stentorian voice. What we like to hear at our dinner meetings, in our church services, on our TV sets and radios, is straightforward speech, conceived in common sense and dedicated to the proposition that we like speakers to talk with, and not at, us.

Despite what many school texts would lead us to believe, public speaking is not a closed art, to be mastered only after years of perfecting the voice and struggling with the mysteries of rhetoric. I have spent almost all of my teaching career proving to people that it is *easy* to speak in public, provided they follow a few simple, but important, rules. When I started to teach at the 125th Street YMCA in New York City back in 1912, I didn't know this any more than my first students knew it. I taught those first classes pretty much the way I had been taught in my college years in Warrensburg, Missouri. But I soon discovered that I was on the wrong track; I was trying to teach adults in the business world as though they were college freshmen. I saw the futility of using Webster, Burke, Pitt and O'Connell as examples to imitate. What the members of my classes wanted was enough courage to stand on their hind legs and make a clear, coherent report at their next business meeting. It wasn't long before I threw the textbooks out the window, got right up there on the podium and, with a few simple ideas, worked with those fellows until they could give their reports in a convincing manner. It worked, because they kept coming back for more.

I wish I could give you a chance to browse through the files of testimonial letters in my home or in the offices of my representatives in various parts of the world. They come from industrial leaders whose names are frequently mentioned in the business section of *The New York Times* and *The Wall Street Journal,* from governors of states and members of parliaments, college presidents, to celebrities in the world of entertainment. There are thousands more from housewives, ministers, teachers, young men and women whose names are not well known yet, even in their own communities, executives and executive trainees, laborers, skilled and unskilled, union men, college students and businesswomen. All of these people felt a need for self-confidence and the ability to express themselves acceptably in public. They were so grateful for having achieved both that they took the time to write me letters of appreciation.

I have seen thousands of similar miracles worked in my courses. I have seen men and women whose lives were transformed by this training, many of them receiving promotions far beyond their dreams or achieving positions of prominence in their business, profession and community. Sometimes this has been done by means of a single talk delivered at the right moment. Let me tell you the story of Mario Lazo.

Years ago, I received a cable from Cuba that astonished me. It read, 'Unless you cable me to the contrary, I am coming to New York to take training to make a speech.' It was signed, 'Mario Lazo'. Who was he? I wondered! I had never heard of him before.

When Mr Lazo arrived in New York, he said, 'The Havana Country Club is going to celebrate the fiftieth birthday of the founder of the club; and I have been invited to present him with a silver cup and to make the principal talk of the evening. Although I am an attorney, I have never made a public talk in my life. I am terrified at the thought of speaking. If I fail, it will be deeply embarrassing to my wife and myself socially; and, in addition, it might lower my prestige with my clients.

That is why I have come all the way from Cuba for your help. I can stay only three weeks.'

During those three weeks, I had Mario Lazo going from one class to another speaking three or four times a night. Three weeks later, he addressed the distinguished gathering at the Havana Country Club. His address was so outstanding that *Time* Magazine reported it under the head of foreign news and described Mario Lazo as a 'silver-tongued orator'.

Sounds like a miracle, doesn't it? It is a miracle—a twentieth-century miracle of conquering fear.

SECOND
Keep Sight of Your Goal

Concentrate your attention on what self-confidence and the ability to talk more effectively will mean to you. Think of what it may mean to you socially, of the friends it will bring, of your increased capacity to be of service in your civic, social or church group, of the influence you will be able to exert in your business. In short, it will prepare you for leadership.

In an article entitled 'Speech and Leadership in Business', S. C. Allyn, Chairman of the Board of the National Cash Register Company and Chairman of UNESCO, wrote in the *Quarterly Journal of Speech*, 'In the history of our business, many a man has drawn attention to himself by a good job done on the platform. A good many years ago a young man, who was then in charge of a small branch in Kansas, gave a rather unusual talk and is today our vice-president in charge of sales.' I happen to know that this vice-president is now the president of the National Cash Register Company.

There is no predicting how far the ability to speak on your feet will take you. One of our graduates, Henry Blackstone,

President of the Servo Corporation of America, says, 'The ability to communicate effectively with others and win their co-operation is an asset we look for in men moving to the top.'

Think of the satisfaction and pleasure that will be yours when you stand up and confidently share your thoughts and feelings with your audience. I have travelled around the world several times, but I know of few things that give greater delight than holding an audience by the power of the spoken word. You get a sense of strength, a feeling of power.

Begin now to picture yourself before an audience you might be called upon to address. See yourself stepping forward with confidence, listen to the hush fall upon the room as you begin, feel the attentive absorption of the audience as you drive home point after point, feel the warmth of the applause as you leave the platform and hear the words of appreciation with which individual members of the audience greet you when the meeting is over. Believe me, there is a magic in it and a never-to-be-forgotten thrill.

William James, Harvard's most distinguished professor of psychology, wrote six sentences that could have a profound effect on your life, six sentences that are the open sesame to Ali Baba's treasure cave of courage, 'In almost any subject, your passion for the subject will save you. If you care enough for a result, you will most certainly attain it. If you wish to be good, you will be good. If you wish to be rich, you will be rich. If you wish to be learned, you will be learned. Only then you must really wish these things and wish them with exclusiveness and not wish one hundred other incompatible things just as strongly.'

Learning to speak effectively to groups brings other benefits than merely the ability to make formal public speeches. As a matter of fact, if you never give a formal public speech in your life, the benefits to be derived from this training are manifold. For one thing, public speaking training is the royal road to self-confidence. Once you realize that you can stand up and talk intelligently to a group of people, it is logical to assume that you can talk to individuals with greater confidence and assurance. Many men and women have taken my course in effective speaking primarily because they were shy and self-conscious in social groups. When they found they were capable of speaking on their feet to their fellow class members without having the roof fall in, they became aware of the ridiculousness of self-consciousness. They began to impress others, their families, friends, business associates, customers and clients, with their newly found poise. Many of our graduates, like Mr Goodrich, were impelled to take the course by the remarkable change in the personalities of those around them.

This type of training also affects the personality in ways that are not immediately apparent. Not long ago I asked Dr David Allman, the Atlantic City surgeon and former president of the American Medical Association, what, in his opinion, were the benefits of public speaking training in terms of mental and physical health. He smiled and said he could best answer that question by writing a prescription that 'no drugstore can fill. It must be filled by the individual; if he thinks he can't, he is wrong.'

I have the prescription on my desk. Every time I read it, I am impressed. Here it is, just as Dr Allman jotted it down,

'Try your best to develop an ability to let others look into your head and heart. Learn to make your thoughts, your ideas, clear to others, individually, in groups, in public. You will find, as you improve in your effort to do this, that you—your real self—are making an impression, an impact, on people such as you never made before.'

You can reap a double benefit from this prescription. Your self-confidence strengthens as you learn to speak to others, and your whole personality grows warmer and better. This means that you are better off emotionally, and if you are better off emotionally, you are better off physically. Public speaking in our modern world is for everybody, men and women, young and elderly. I do not know personally about its advantages to one in business or industry. I only hear that they are great. But I do know its advantages in health. Speak when you can, to a few or to many; you will do it better and better, as I have found out, myself; and you will feel a buoyancy of spirit, a sense of being a whole, rounded person, such as you never felt before.

It is a wonderful sense to have, and no pill ever made can give it to you.

The second guidepost, then, is to picture yourself as successfully doing what now you fear to do, and to concentrate on the benefits you will receive through your ability to talk acceptably before groups. Remember the words of William James, 'If you care enough for a result, you will most certainly attain it.'

THIRD
Predetermine Your Mind to Success

I was asked once, on a radio program, to tell in three sentences the most important lesson I have ever learned. This is what I said, 'The biggest lesson I have ever learned is the stupendous importance of what we think. If I knew what you think, I would know what you are, for your thoughts make you what you are. By changing our thoughts, we can change our lives.'

You have set your sights on the goal of increased confidence and more effective communication. From now on, you must think positively, not negatively, about your chances to succeed in this endeavour. You must develop a buoyant optimism about the outcome of your efforts to speak before groups. You must set the seal of determination upon every word and action that you devote toward the development of this ability.

Here is a story that is dramatic proof of the need for resolute determination on the part of anyone who wants to meet the challenge of more expressive speaking. The man I am writing about has come up the management ladder so far that he has become a big business legend. But the first time he stood up to speak in college, words failed him. He couldn't get beyond the middle of the five-minute talk his teacher had assigned. His face went white, and he hurried off the platform in tears.

The man who had that experience as a young student didn't let that failure frustrate him. He determined to become a good speaker and didn't stop in that determination until he became a world-respected economic consultant to the government. His name is Clarence B. Randall. In one of his thoughtful books, *Freedom's Faith,* he has this to say about public speaking, 'I have service stripes all the way up one sleeve and all the way down the other from appearances before luncheons and dinners of manufacturers' associations, Chambers of Commerce, Rotary Clubs, fund-raising campaigns, alumni organizations and all the rest. I talked myself into World War I by a patriotic address in Escanaba, Michigan; I have barnstormed for charity with Mickey Rooney and for education with President James Bryant Conant of Harvard and Chancellor Robert M. Hutchins of the University of Chicago; and I have even made an after-dinner speech in very bad French.

'I think I know something about what an audience will listen to, and how they want it said. *And there is nothing whatever about it that a man worthy to bear important business responsibility cannot learn if he will.*'

I agree with Mr Randall. The will to succeed must be a vital part of the process of becoming an effective speaker. If I could look into your mind and ascertain the strength of your desire and the light and shadow of your thought I could foretell, almost with certainty, the swiftness of your progress toward your goal of improved communicative skills.

In one of my classes in the Middle West, a man stood up the first night and unabashedly said that as a builder of homes he wouldn't be content until he became a spokesman for the American Home Builders' Association. He wanted nothing more than to go up and down this country and tell everybody he met the problems and achievements of his industry. Joe Haverstick meant what he said. He was the kind of class member that delights an instructor: he was in dead earnest. He wanted to be able to talk, not on local issues only, but on national ones, and there was no half-heartedness about his desires. He prepared his talks thoroughly, practiced them carefully, and never missed a single session, though it was the busy season of the year for men in his business. He did precisely what such a class member always does—he progressed at a rate that surprised him. In two months he had become one of the outstanding members of the class.

The instructor handling that class was in Norfolk, Virginia, about a year later, and this is what he wrote, 'I had forgotten all about Joe Haverstick back in Ohio when, one morning while I was having breakfast, I opened the *Virginia Pilot*. There was a picture of Joe and a write-up about him. The night before, he had addressed a large meeting of area builders, and I saw that Joe was not just a spokesman for the National Home Builders' Association; he was its president.'

So, to succeed in this work, you need the qualities that are essential in any worthwhile endeavour: desire amounting to enthusiasm, persistence to wear away mountains and the self-assurance to believe you will succeed.

POINTS TO REMEMBER

1. There is no 'born' public speaker.
2. Decide on a goal and never lose sight of it.
3. Your mental attitude determines your success.

7

APPLYING WHAT YOU HAVE LEARNED

Perhaps you are wondering when to begin applying what you have learned in the previous chapters of this book. You may be surprised if I answer that query by one word: immediately.

Even though you are not planning to make a speech in public for some time, if at all, I am certain you will find that the principles and techniques in this book are applicable every day. When I say start using these techniques *now*, I mean in the very next speaking situation in which you find yourself.

If you analyse the speaking that you do every day, you will be amazed by the similarity of purpose between your daily speaking and the type of formal communication discussed in these pages.

In daily speaking, these purposes are fluid, merging with one another and constantly changing through the course of the day. At one moment we may be indulging in friendly chitchat and then suddenly we may be using speech to sell a product or persuade a child to put his spending money in the bank. By applying the techniques described in this book to everyday conversation we can make ourselves more effective, get our ideas across more efficiently and motivate others with skill and fact.

FIRST
Use Specific Detail in Everyday Conversation

Take just one of these techniques, for instance. I appeal to you to put detail in your talk. In that way you make your ideas come alive, in a vivid and graphic way. The use of detail is just as important in everyday conversation. Just think for a moment of the really interesting conversationalists of your acquaintance. Aren't they the ones who fill their talk with colourful, dramatic details, who have the ability to use picturesque speech?

Before you can begin to develop your conversational skills you must have confidence. So almost all that was said in the first three chapters of this book will be useful in giving you the security to mix with others and to voice your opinions in an informal social group. Once you are eager to express your ideas even on a limited scale, you will begin to search your experience for material that can be converted to conversation. Here a wonderful thing happens—your horizons begin to expand and you see your life take on new meaning.

Housewives, whose interests may have become somewhat restricted, have been most enthusiastic in reporting what happens when they begin to apply their knowledge of speaking techniques to small conversational groups. 'I realize that my newly found confidence gave me courage to speak up at social functions,' Mrs R. D. Hart told her classmates in Cincinnati, 'and I began taking an interest in current events. Instead of withdrawing from the give and take of the group I eagerly joined it. Not only that, but everything I did became grist for the conversational mill and I found myself becoming interested in a host of new activities.'

To an educator there is nothing new in Mrs Hart's grateful report. Once the drive to learn and to apply what has been learned is stimulated, it starts a whole train of action and interaction that vivifies the entire personality. A cycle of achievement is set up and, like Mrs Hart, one gets the feeling of fulfilment, all through putting into practice just one of the principles taught in this book.

Though few of us are professional teachers, all of us use speech to inform others on many occasions during the day. As parents instructing our children, as neighbours explaining a new method of pruning roses, as tourists exchanging ideas on the best route to follow, we constantly find ourselves in conversational situations that require clarity and coherence of thought, vitality and vigour of expression.

SECOND
Use Effective Speaking Techniques in Your Job

Now we enter the area of the communicative process as it affects our jobs. As salesmen, managers, clerks, department heads, group leaders, teachers, ministers, nurses, executives, doctors, lawyers, accountants and engineers, we are all charged with the responsibility of explaining specialized areas of knowledge and giving professional instructions. Our ability to make these instructions in clear, concise language may often be the yardstick used by our superiors in judging our competence. How to think quickly and verbalize adroitly is a skill acquired in presenting speeches of information, but this skill is by no means limited to formal speaking—it can be used every day by every one of us. The need for clarity in business and professional speech today is highlighted by the recent spate of oral communications courses in industry, government and professional organizations.

THIRD
Seek Opportunities to Speak in Public

In addition to using the principles of this book in everyday speech, where incidentally you will reap the greatest rewards, you should seek every opportunity to speak in public. How do you do this? By joining a club where public speaking of some sort goes on. Don't just be an inactive member, a mere looker-on. Pitch in and help by doing committee work. Most of these jobs go begging. Get to be program chairman. That will give you an opportunity to interview good speakers in your community, and you certainly will be called upon to make speeches of introduction.

As soon as possible, develop a twenty- to thirty-minute talk. Use the suggestions in this book as a guide. Let your club or organization know that you are prepared to address them. Offer your services to a speaker's bureau in your town. Fund-raising campaigns are looking for volunteers to speak for them. They provide you with a speaker's kit which will be of great help in preparing your talk. Many speakers of consequence have begun in this way. Some of them have risen to great prominence. Take Sam Levenson, for example, the radio and TV star and a speaker whose services are sought all over the country. He was a high school teacher in New York. Just as a sideliner, he began making short talks about what he knew best, his family, relatives, his students and the unusual aspects of his job. These talks took fire, and he was soon asked to address so many groups it began to interfere with his teaching chores. But, by this time he was a guest on network programs and it wasn't long before Sam Levenson transferred his talents entirely to the entertainment world.

FOURTH
You Must Persist

When we learn any new thing, like French or golf or speaking in public, we never advance steadily. We do not improve gradually. We do it by waves, by abrupt starts and sudden stops. Then we remain stationary a time, or we may even slip back and lose some of the ground we have previously gained. These periods of stagnation, or retrogression, are well known by all psychologists; they have been named 'plateaus in the curve of learning'. Students of effective speaking will sometimes be stalled, perhaps for weeks, on one of these plateaus. Work as hard as they may, they cannot seem to get off it. The weak ones give up in despair. Those with grit persist, and they find that suddenly, almost overnight, without knowing how or why it has happened, they have made great progress. They have lifted from the plateau like an airplane. Abruptly they have acquired naturalness, force and confidence in their speaking.

You may always, as has been stated elsewhere in these pages, experience some fleeting fear, some shock, some nervous anxiety, the first few moments you face an audience. Even the greatest musicians have felt it in spite of their innumerable public appearances. Paderewski always fidgeted nervously with his cuffs immediately before he sat down at the piano. But as soon as he began to play, all of his audience-fear vanished quickly like a mist in August sunshine.

His experience will be yours. If you will but persevere, you will soon eradicate everything, including this initial fear; and that will be initial fear, and nothing more. After the first few sentences, you will have control of yourself. You will be speaking with positive pleasure.

One time a young man who aspired to study law wrote

to Lincoln for advice. Lincoln replied, 'If you are resolutely determined to make a lawyer of yourself, the thing is more than half done already… Always bear in mind that your own resolution to succeed is more important than any other one thing.'

Lincoln knew. He had gone through it all. He had never, in his entire life, had more than a total of one year's schooling. And books? Lincoln once said he had walked and borrowed every book within fifty miles of his home. A log fire was usually kept going all night in the cabin. Sometimes he read by the light of that fire. There were cracks between the logs in the cabin, and Lincoln often kept a book sticking there. As soon as it was light enough to read in the morning, he rolled over on his bed of leaves, rubbed his eyes, pulled out the book and began devouring it.

He walked twenty and thirty miles to hear a speaker and, returning home, he practiced his talks everywhere—in the fields, in the woods, before the crowds gathered at Jones' grocery at Gentryville; he joined literary and debating societies in New Salem and Springfield, and practiced speaking on the topics of the day. He was shy in the presence of women; when he courted Mary Todd he used to sit in the parlour, bashful and silent, unable to find words, listening while she did the talking. Yet that was the man who, by faithful practice and home study, made himself into the speaker who debated with the most accomplished orator of his day, Senator Douglas. This was the man who, at Gettysburg, and again in his second inaugural address, rose to heights of eloquence that have rarely been attained in all the annals of mankind.

Small wonder that, in view of his own terrific handicaps and pitiful struggle, Lincoln wrote, 'If you are resolutely determined to make a lawyer out of yourself, the thing is more than half done already.'

An excellent picture of Abraham Lincoln hangs in the President's office in the White House. 'Often when I had some matter to decide,' said Theodore Roosevelt, 'something involved and difficult to dispose of, something where there were conflicting rights and interest, I would look up at Lincoln, try to imagine him in my place, try to figure out what he would do in the same circumstances. It may sound odd to you, but, frankly, it seemed to make my troubles easier of solution.'

Why not try Roosevelt's plan? Why not, if you are discouraged and feeling like giving up the fight to make a more effective speaker of yourself, why not ask yourself what he would do under the circumstances? You know what he would do. You know what he did do. After he had been beaten by Stephen A. Douglas in the race for the U.S. Senate, he admonished his followers not to 'give up after one or one hundred defeats.'

FIFTH
Keep the Certainty of Reward Before You

How I wish I could get you to prop this book open on your breakfast table every morning until you had memorized these words from Professor William James:

> Let no youth have any anxiety about the upshot of his education, whatever the line of it may be. If he keeps faithfully busy each hour of the working day, he may safely leave the final result to itself. He can, with perfect certainty, count on waking up some fine morning to find himself one of the competent ones of his generation, in whatever pursuit he may have singled out.

I have known and carefully watched literally thousands of persons trying to gain self-confidence and the ability to talk in public. Those that succeeded were, in only a few instances, persons of unusual brilliancy. For the most part, they were the ordinary run of businessmen you will find in your own home town. But they kept on. More exceptional men sometimes got discouraged or too deeply immersed in money-making, and they did not get very far; but the ordinary individual with grit and singleness of purpose, at the end of the road, was at the top.

That is only human and natural. Don't you see the same tiling occurring all the time in commerce and the professions? John D. Rockefeller, Sr., said that the first essential for success in business was patience and the knowledge that reward is ultimately certain. It is likewise one of the first essentials for success in effective speaking.

If you put enthusiasm into learning how to speak more effectively you will find that the obstacles in your path will disappear. This is a challenge to focus all your talent and power on the goal of effective communication with your fellow men. Think of the self-reliance, the assurance, the poise that will be yours, the sense of mastery that comes from being able to hold the attention, stir the emotions and convince a group to act. You will find that competence in self-expression will lead to competence in other ways as well, for training in effective speaking is the royal road to self-confidence in all the areas of working and living.

In the manual for the guidance of instructors who teach the Dale Carnegie Course are these words, 'When class members discover that they can hold the attention of an audience and receive an instructor's praise, and the applause of the class—when they are able to do that, they develop a sense of inner power, courage and calm that they have never before experienced. The result? They undertake and accomplish things that they never dreamed possible. They find themselves longing to talk before groups. They take active part in business and professional and community activities, and become leaders.'

The word 'leadership' has been used often in the chapters that have gone before this one. Clear, forceful and emphatic expressiveness is one of the marks of leadership in our society. This expressiveness must govern all the utterances of the leader from private interview to public pronouncements. Properly applied, the material in this book will help to develop leadership—in the family, the church group, the civic organization, the corporation and the government.

POINTS TO REMEMBER

1. Practice speaking every day and analyse it.
2. Use effective speaking techniques in your job.
3. Keep working hard and don't give up. You will see the results yourself.

8

CREATING A POSITIVE MENTAL ATTITUDE

Mental attitude. The power we hold in our heads. The way reality can be changed dramatically by a single solitary thought. It sounds a little hard to believe. 'Think happy thoughts, and you will be happy. Think successful thoughts, and you will succeed.' Or from the ice at Madison Square Garden, 'Convert that huge wall of hostility into a source of positive strength.' Denis Potvin knew the power of attitude. The old expression had it wrong: it isn't what you eat that determines what you are. *You are what you think.*

Contrary to what most people want to believe, outside influences do not usually determine personal happiness. What matters is how we react to those influences, good or bad.

Humour is vital. Never forget that this simple element helps maintain perspective. Welty agrees. 'Keep it in perspective,' he advises. 'When things don't seem to be going well, relax, take your time. Think about what's going on and your reaction to it. Tell yourself, "Back up ten yards, and see how we go at the next play."'

There are hundreds of things that can irritate, worry or annoy you. Don't let them. Don't let the small things get you down.

'When you get cut off on the freeway, there are only two things you can do,' says Ted Owen, publisher of the *San Diego Business Journal*, who like most Southern Californians spends an awful lot of time behind the wheel. 'You can swear at the other driver and give some obscene gesture, or you can shrug and say to yourself, "How long is it going to take this guy to end up in the junk heap? He's not going to make it to work the way he's driving."'

Neither approach will have much effect on how quickly you arrive at the office. Shrugging at this trivial irritation will get you there in a much happier and more productive frame of mind. It might even add a couple of years to your life.

Owen wasn't born with this laissez-faire outlook on life. He used to have one of those high-tension personalities, but he came over the years to recognize how self-destructive it could be. When he was asked to run the *Business Journal*, where he would be commenting frequently on how other executives perform, he decided he'd better overcome his own attitude problems.

'Many of us tend to be reactive and overreactive,' he observes. 'Since starting this job, I've never been angry at work. I got angry other places, but I haven't been angry here.' People are responding like they've never responded before.

After years of struggle, things were finally looking up for Mary Kay Ash. She had remarried.

The children were finally grown. She and her new husband had saved just enough money to start a small cosmetics company, a dream she had nurtured for years.

Then her dream nearly disintegrated. 'The day before we were to open this company,' Ash recalls, 'my husband died of a heart attack right there at the breakfast table. My husband was to handle the administration of the company. I don't know a thing about administration, even today. Every single penny was committed. We had only five thousand dollars, my personal savings. It sounds like very little, but probably it would be worth fifty thousand today.

'On the day of the funeral, we had no time to waste. My two sons and my daughter and I sat down to decide what to do. Do I stop or do I go on? All my dreams just plunged to the ground.'

But Mary Kay Ash believed in herself too much to give up. Her son Richard, who was just twenty, offered to do what he could. 'Mother,' he said, 'I'll move to Dallas to help you.'

She had her doubts. 'I thought, "Big deal." How would you like to turn your life savings over to a twenty-year-old? I figured maybe he could lift boxes I couldn't. I didn't know if he could fill out an order or not. I mean, he had been just one kid that I had to bring up by myself.'

But Ash wasn't one to let doubt overwhelm her. She doesn't take well to defeat. So she pressed on. 'That was the beginning of the company. True to his word, Richard moved to Dallas the very next day with his little two-month bride on his arm. The lawyers were saying, "Why don't you go directly to the trash and throw the money in, because you're never going to make it." And pamphlets from Washington told us how many cosmetics companies go broke every morning.'

Her positive attitude got her through it all. She just kept telling herself, 'I think that people will support that which they have to create. I think it can be done, and I'm going to try.' With an attitude like that, is it any surprise that Ash succeeded?

These positive, self-confident feelings don't only help you achieve more. They also make other people want to be associated with you. We all respond to the attitudes of others. That's why people are drawn to those with upbeat outlooks on life. We want to surround ourselves with friends or co-workers who are happy and productive, who have a can-do, it's-no-problem attitude. Just as predictably, the constant complainer in any crowd doesn't get much company.

Why is this? Attitude rubs off on others, good or bad. This is a vital concept to remember for anyone who wants to be a successful leader today. There are few more powerful motivators than a positive attitude.

We all know organizations where a large percentage of the employees are unhappy. How did they get that way? Slowly, one employee at a time. A leader has to fight that spread, constantly substituting positive feelings and attitudes for negative ones.

POINTS TO REMEMBER

1. Attaining a balanced life is more productive and satisfying.
2. Only a good person can be a good leader.
3. Achieving a reasonable balance between work and leisure is the greatest challenge.

9

REMEMBER THAT NO ONE EVER KICKS A DEAD DOG

An event occurred in 1929 that created a national sensation in educational circles. Learned men from all over America rushed to Chicago to witness the affair. A few years earlier, a young man by the name of Robert Hutchins had worked his way through Yale, acting as a waiter, a lumberjack, a tutor, and a clothesline salesman. Now, only eight years later, he was being inaugurated as president of the fourth richest university in America, the University of Chicago. His age? Thirty. Incredible! The older educators shook their heads. Criticism came roaring down upon this 'boy wonder' like a rockslide. He was this and he was that—too young, inexperienced—his educational ideas were cockeyed. Even the newspapers joined in the attack.

The day he was inaugurated, a friend said to the father of Robert Maynard Hutchins, 'I was shocked this morning to read that newspaper editorial denouncing your son.'

'Yes,' the elder Hutchins replied, 'it was severe, but remember that no one ever kicks a dead dog.'

Yes, and the more important a dog is, the more satisfaction people get in kicking him. The Prince of Wales who later became Edward VIII (now the Duke of Windsor) had that brought home to him in the seat of his pants. He was attending Dartmouth College in Devonshire at the time—a college that corresponds to our Naval Academy at Annapolis. The Prince was about fourteen. One day one of the naval officers found him crying, and asked him what was wrong. He refused to tell at first, but finally admitted the truth: he was being kicked by the naval cadets. The commodore of the college summoned the boys and explained to them that the Prince had not complained, but he wanted to find out why the Prince had been singled out for this rough treatment.

After much hemming and hawing and toe scraping, the cadets finally confessed that when they themselves became commanders and captains in the King's Navy, they wanted to be able to say that they had kicked the King!

So when you are kicked and criticized, remember that it is often done because it gives the kicker a feeling of importance. It often means that you are accomplishing something and are worthy of attention. Many people get a sense of savage satisfaction out of denouncing those who are better educated than they are or more successful. For example, while I was writing this chapter, I received a letter from a woman denouncing General William Booth, founder of the Salvation Army. I had given a laudatory broadcast about General Booth; so this woman wrote me, saying that General Booth had stolen eight million dollars of the money he had collected to help poor people. The charge, of course, was absurd. But this woman wasn't looking for truth. She was seeking the mean-spirited gratification that she got from tearing down someone far above her. I threw her bitter letter into the wastebasket, and thanked Almighty God that I wasn't married to her. Her letter didn't tell me anything at all about General Booth, but it did tell me a lot about her. Schopenhauer had said it years ago, 'Vulgar people take huge delight in the faults and follies of great men.'

One hardly thinks of the president of Yale as a vulgar man; yet a former president of Yale, Timothy Dwight, apparently took huge delight in denouncing a man who was running for President of the United States. The president of Yale warned that if this man were elected President, 'we may see our wives and daughters the victims of legal prostitution, soberly dishonoured, speciously polluted; the outcasts of delicacy and virtue, the loathing of God and man.'

Sounds almost like a denunciation of Hitler, doesn't it? But it wasn't. It was a denunciation of Thomas Jefferson. *Which* Thomas Jefferson? Surely not the *immortal* Thomas Jefferson, the author of the Declaration of Independence, the patron saint of democracy? Yea, verily, that was the man.

What American do you suppose was denounced as a 'hypocrite', 'an impostor', and as 'little better than a murderer'? A newspaper cartoon depicted him on a guillotine, the big knife ready to cut off his head. Crowds jeered at him and hissed him as he rode through the streets. Who was he? George Washington.

But that occurred a long time ago. Maybe human nature has improved since then. Let's see. Let's take the case of Admiral Peary—the explorer who startled and thrilled the world by reaching the North Pole with dog sleds on April 6, 1909—a goal that brave men for centuries had suffered and starved and died to attain. Peary himself almost died from cold and starvation; and eight of his toes were frozen so hard they had to be cut off. He was so overwhelmed with disasters that he feared he would go insane. His superior naval officers in Washington were burned up because Peary was getting so much publicity and acclaim. So they accused him of collecting money for scientific expeditions and then 'lying around and loafing in the Arctic'.

And they probably believed it because it is almost impossible not to believe what you want to believe. Their determination to humiliate and block Peary was so violent that only a direct order from President McKinley enabled Peary to continue his career in the Arctic.

Would Peary have been denounced if he had had a desk job in the Navy Department in Washington? No. He wouldn't have been important enough then to have aroused jealousy.

General Grant had an even worse experience than Admiral Peary. In 1862, General Grant won the first great decisive victory that the North had enjoyed—a victory that was achieved in one afternoon, a victory that made Grant a national idol overnight—a victory that had tremendous repercussions even in far-off Europe—a victory that set church bells ringing and bonfires blazing from Maine to the banks of the Mississippi. Yet within six weeks after achieving that great victory, Grant—hero of the North—was *arrested and his army was taken from him. He wept with humiliation and despair.*

Why was General U. S. Grant arrested at the flood tide of his victory? Largely because he had aroused the jealousy and envy of his arrogant superiors.

POINTS TO REMEMBER

1. The more you succeed, the more enemies you will make.
2. People often try to bring others down in order to feel important.
3. Recognize the compliment behind the criticism.

10

THE BIG SECRET OF DEALING WITH PEOPLE

There is only one way under high heaven to get anybody to do anything. Did you ever stop to think of that? Yes, just one way. And that is by making the other person want to do it.

Remember, there is no other way.

Of course, you can make someone want to give you his watch by sticking a revolver in his ribs. You can make your employees give you cooperation—until your back is turned—by threatening to fire them. You can make a child do what you want it to do by a whip or a threat. But these crude methods have sharply undesirable repercussions.

The only way I can get you to do anything is by giving you what you want.

What do you want?

Sigmund Freud said that everything you and I do springs from two motives: the sex urge and the desire to be great.

John Dewey, one of America's most profound philosophers, phrased it a bit differently. Dr Dewey said that the deepest urge in human nature is 'the desire to be important'. Remember that phrase, 'the desire to be important.' It is significant.

What do you want? Not many things, but the few things

that you do wish, you crave with an insistence that will not be denied. Some of the things most people want include:

1. Health and the preservation of life.
2. Food.
3. Sleep.
4. Money and the things money will buy.
5. Life in the hereafter.
6. Sexual gratification.
7. The well-being of our children.
8. A feeling of importance.

Almost all these wants are usually gratified—all except one. But there is one longing—almost as deep, almost as imperious, as the desire for food or sleep—which is seldom gratified. It is what Freud calls 'the desire to be great'. It is what Dewey calls the 'desire to be important'.

The desire for a feeling of importance is one of the chief distinguishing differences between mankind and the animals. To illustrate: when I was a farm boy out in Missouri, my father bred fine Duroc-Jersey hogs and pedigreed white-faced cattle. We used to exhibit our hogs and white-faced cattle at the country fairs and livestock shows throughout the Middle West. We won first prizes by the score. My father pinned his blue ribbons on a sheet of white muslin, and when friends or visitors came to the house, he would get out the long sheet of muslin. He would hold one end and I would hold the other while he exhibited the blue ribbons.

The hogs didn't care about the ribbons they had won. But Father did. These prizes gave him a feeling of importance.

If our ancestors hadn't had this flaming urge for a feeling of importance, civilisation would have been impossible. Without it, we should have been just about like animals.

It was this desire for a feeling of importance that led an uneducated, poverty-stricken grocery clerk to study some law books he found in the bottom of a barrel of household plunder that he had bought for fifty cents. You have probably heard of this grocery clerk. His name was Lincoln.

It was this desire for a feeling of importance that inspired Dickens to write his immortal novels. This desire inspired Sir Christopher Wren to design his symphonies in stone. This desire made Rockefeller amass millions that he never spent! And this same desire made the richest family in your town build a house far too large for its requirements.

This desire makes you want to wear the latest styles, drive the latest cars and talk about your brilliant children.

It is this desire that lures many boys and girls into joining gangs and engaging in criminal activities. 'The average young criminal,' according to E.P. Mulrooney, onetime police commissioner of New York, 'is filled with ego, and his first request after arrest is for those lurid newspapers that make him out a hero. The disagreeable prospect of serving time seems remote so long as he can gloat over his likeness sharing space with pictures of sports figures, movie and TV stars and politicians.'

If you tell me how you get your feeling of importance, I'll tell you what you are. That determines your character. That is the most significant thing about you. For example, John D. Rockefeller got his feeling of importance by giving money to erect a modern hospital in Peking, China, to care for millions of poor people whom he had never seen and never would see. Dillinger, on the other hand, got his feeling of importance by being a bandit, a bank robber and killer. When the FBI agents were hunting him, he dashed into a farmhouse up in Minnesota and said, 'I'm Dillinger!' He was proud of the fact that he was

Public Enemy Number One. 'I'm not going to hurt you, but I'm Dillinger!' he said.

Yes, the one significant difference between Dillinger and Rockefeller is how they got their feeling of importance.

YOU DON'T HAVE TO BE A CELEBRITY TO FEEL IMPORTANT

History sparkles with amusing examples of famous people struggling for a feeling of importance. Even George Washington wanted to be called 'His Mightiness, the President of the United States'; and Columbus pleaded for the title 'Admiral of the Ocean and Viceroy of India'. Catherine the Great refused to open letters that were not addressed to 'Her Imperial Majesty'; and Mrs Lincoln, in the White House, turned upon Mrs Grant like a tigress and shouted, 'How dare you be seated in my presence until I invite you!'

Our millionaires helped finance Admiral Byrd's expedition to the Antarctic in 1928 with the understanding that ranges of icy mountains would be named after them; and Victor Hugo aspired to have nothing less than the city of Paris renamed in his honour. Even Shakespeare, mightiest of the mighty, tried to add lustre to his name by procuring a coat of arms for his family.

People sometimes become invalids in order to win sympathy and attention, and get a feeling of importance. For example, take Mrs McKinley. She got a feeling of importance by forcing her husband, the President of the United States, to neglect important affairs of state while he reclined on the bed beside her for hours at a time, his arm about her, soothing her to sleep. She fed her gnawing desire for attention by insisting that he remain with her while she was having her teeth fixed, and once created a stormy scene when he had to leave her alone with the dentist while he kept an appointment with John Hay, his secretary of state.

If some people are so hungry for a feeling of importance that they actually go insane to get it, imagine what miracle you and I can achieve by giving people honest appreciation this side of insanity.

When a study was made a few years ago on runaway wives, what do you think was discovered to be the main reason wives ran away? It was 'lack of appreciation'. And I'd bet that a similar study made of runaway husbands would come out the same way. We often take our spouses so much for granted that we never let them know we appreciate them.

A member of one of our classes told of a request made by his wife. She and a group of other women in her church were involved in a self-improvement programme. She asked her husband to help her by listing six things he believed she could do to help her become a better wife. He reported to the class, 'I was surprised by such a request. Frankly, it would have been easy for me to list six things I would like to change about her—my heavens, she could have listed a thousand things she would like to change about me—but I didn't. I said to her, "Let me think about it and give you an answer in the morning."

'The next morning, I got up very early and called the florist and had them send six red roses to my wife with a note saying, "I can't think of six things I would like to change about you. I love you the way you are."

'When I arrived at home that evening, who do you think greeted me at the door? That's right. My wife! She was almost in tears. Needless to say, I was extremely glad I had not criticised her as she had requested.

'The following Sunday at church, after she had reported the results of her assignment, several women with whom she had been studying came up to me and said, "That was the most considerate thing I have ever heard." It was then I realised the power of appreciation.'

Florenz Ziegfeld, the most spectacular producer who ever dazzled Broadway, gained his reputation by his subtle ability to 'glorify the American girl'. Time after time, he took drab little creatures that no one ever looked at twice and transformed them on the stage into glamorous visions of mystery and seduction. Knowing the value of appreciation and confidence, he made women feel beautiful by the sheer power of his gallantry and consideration. He was practical: he raised the salary of chorus girls from $30 a week to as high as $175. And he was also chivalrous; on opening night at the Follies, he sent telegrams to the stars in the cast, and he deluged every chorus girl in the show with American Beauty roses.

I once succumbed to the fad of fasting and went for six days and nights without eating. It wasn't difficult. I was less hungry at the end of the sixth day than I was at the end of the second. Yet I know, as you know, people who would think they had committed a crime if they let their families or employees go for six days without food; but they will let them go for six days, and six weeks, and sometimes sixty years without giving them the hearty appreciation that they crave almost as much as they crave food.

When Alfred Lunt, one of the great actors of his time, played the leading role in *Reunion in Vienna*, he said, 'There is nothing I need so much as nourishment for my self-esteem.'

We nourish the bodies of our children and friends and employees, but how seldom do we nourish their self-esteem? We provide them with roast beef and potatoes to build energy, but we neglect to give them kind words of appreciation that would sing in their memories for years like the music of the morning stars.

Some readers are saying right now as they read these lines, 'Oh, phooey! *Flattery! Bear oil!* I've tried that stuff. It doesn't work—not with intelligent people.'

Of course flattery seldom works with discerning people. It is shallow, selfish and insincere. It ought to fail and it usually does. True, some people are so hungry, so thirsty, for appreciation that they will swallow anything, just as a starving man will eat grass and fishworms.

Even Queen Victoria was susceptible to flattery. Prime Minister Benjamin Disraeli confessed that he put it on thick in dealing with the Queen. To use his exact words, he said he, 'spread it on with a trowel'. But Disraeli was one of the most polished, deft and adroit men who ever ruled the far-flung British Empire. He was a genius in his line. What would work for him wouldn't necessarily work for you and me. In the long run, flattery will do you more harm than good. Flattery is counterfeit, and like counterfeit money, it will eventually get you into trouble if you pass it to someone else.

The difference between appreciation and flattery? That is simple. One is sincere and the other insincere. One comes from the heart out; the other from the teeth out. One is unselfish; the other selfish. One is universally admired; the other universally condemned.

I recently saw a bust of Mexican hero General Alvaro Obregon in the Chapultepec palace in Mexico City. Below the bust are carved these wise words from General Obregon's philosophy, 'Don't be afraid of enemies who attack you. Be afraid of the friends who flatter you.'

No! No! No! I am not suggesting flattery! Far from it. I'm talking about a new way of life. Let me repeat. *I am talking about a new way of life.*

King George V had a set of six maxims displayed on the

walls of his study at Buckingham Palace. One of these maxims said, 'Teach me neither to proffer nor receive cheap praise.' That's all flattery is—cheap praise. I once read a definition of flattery that may be worth repeating, 'Flattery is telling the other person precisely what he thinks about himself.'

'Use what language you will,' said Ralph Waldo Emerson, 'you can never say anything but what you are.'

If all we had to do was flatter, everybody would catch on and we should all be experts in human relations.

When we are not engaged in thinking about some definite problem, we usually spend about 95 per cent of our time thinking about ourselves. Now, if we stop thinking about ourselves for a while and begin to think of the other person's good points, we won't have to resort to flattery so cheap and false that it can be spotted almost before it is out of the mouth.

One of the most neglected virtues of our daily existence is appreciation. Somehow, we neglect to praise our son or daughter when he or she brings home a good report card, and we fail to encourage our children when they first succeed in baking a cake or building a birdhouse. Nothing pleases children more than this kind of parental interest and approval.

The next time you enjoy filet mignon at the club, send word to the chef that it was excellently prepared, and when a tired salesperson shows you unusual courtesy, please mention it.

Every minister, lecturer and public speaker knows the discouragement of pouring himself or herself out to an audience and not receiving a single ripple of appreciative comment. What applies to professionals applies doubly to workers in offices, shops and factories and our families and friends. In our interpersonal relations we should never forget that all our associates are human beings and hunger for appreciation. It is the legal tender that all souls enjoy.

Try leaving a friendly trail of little sparks of gratitude on your daily trips. You will be surprised how they will set small flames of friendship that will be rose beacons on your next visit.

Pamela Dunham of New Fairfield, Connecticut, had among her responsibilities on her job the supervision of a janitor who was doing a very poor job. The other employees would jeer at him and litter the hallways to show him what a bad job he was doing. It was so bad, productive time was being lost in the shop.

Without success, Pam tried various ways to motivate this person. She noticed that occasionally he did a particularly good piece of work. She made a point to praise him for it in front of the other people. Each day the job he did all around got better, and pretty soon he started doing all his work efficiently. Now he does an excellent job and other people give him appreciation and recognition. Honest appreciation got results where criticism and ridicule failed.

Hurting people not only does not change them, it is never called for. There is an old saying that I have cut out and pasted on my mirror where I cannot help but see it every day:

> I shall pass this way but once; any good, therefore, that I can do or any kindness that I can show to any human being, let me do it now. Let me not defer nor neglect it, for I shall not pass this way again.

Emerson said, 'Every man I meet is my superior in some way. In that, I learn of him.'

If that was true of Emerson, isn't it likely to be a thousand times more true of you and me? Let's cease thinking of our accomplishments, our wants. Let's try to figure out the other person's good points. Then forget flattery. Give honest, sincere appreciation. Be 'hearty in your approbation and lavish in your praise' and people will cherish your words and treasure them and repeat them over a lifetime—repeat them years after you have forgotten them.

> **POINTS TO REMEMBER**
>
> 1. The only way you can get someone to do anything is by giving them what they want.
> 2. The 'craving' to be appreciated is universal.
> 3. Honest appreciation gets results where criticism and ridicule fail.

11

MAKE A GOOD FIRST IMPRESSION

At a dinner party in New York, one of the guests, a woman who had inherited money, was eager to make a pleasing impression on everyone. She had squandered a modest fortune on sables, diamonds and pearls. But she hadn't done anything whatever about her face. It radiated sourness and selfishness. She didn't realise what everyone knows: namely, that the expression one wears on one's face is far more important than the clothes one wears on one's back.

Charles Schwab told me his smile had been worth a million dollars. And he was probably understating the truth. For Schwab's personality, his charm, his ability to make people like him, were almost wholly responsible for his extraordinary success; and one of the most delightful factors in his personality was his captivating smile.

Actions speak louder than words, and a smile says, 'I like you. You make me happy. I am glad to see you.'

That is why dogs make such a hit. They are so glad to see us that they almost jump out of their skins. So, naturally, we are glad to see them.

A baby's smile has the same effect.

Have you ever been in a doctor's waiting room and looked around at all the glum faces waiting impatiently to be seen? Dr

Stephen K. Sproul, a veterinarian in Raytown, Missouri, told of a typical spring day when his waiting room was full of clients waiting to have their pets inoculated. No one was talking to anyone else, and all were probably thinking of a dozen other things they would rather be doing than 'wasting time' sitting in that office. He told one of our classes, 'There were six or seven clients waiting when a young woman came in with a nine-months-old baby and a kitten. As luck would have it, she sat down next to a gentleman who was more than a little distraught about the long wait for service. The next thing he knew, the baby just looked up at him with that great big smile that is so characteristic of babies. What did that gentleman do? Just what you and I would do, of course; he smiled back at the baby. Soon he struck up a conversation with the woman about her baby and his grandchildren, and soon the entire reception room joined in, and the boredom and tension were converted into a pleasant and enjoyable experience.'

An insincere grin? No. That doesn't fool anybody. We know it is mechanical and we resent it. I am talking about a real smile, a heart-warming smile, a smile that comes from within, the kind of smile that will bring a good price in the marketplace.

Professor James V. McConnell, a psychologist at the University of Michigan, expressed his feelings about a smile. 'People who smile,' he said, 'tend to manage, teach and sell more effectively, and to raise happier children. There's far more information in a smile than a frown. That's why encouragement is a much more effective teaching device than punishment.'

The employment manager of a large New York department store told me she would rather hire a sales clerk who hadn't finished grade school, if he or she has a pleasant smile, than to hire a doctor of philosophy with a sombre face.

The effect of a smile is powerful—even when it is unseen.

Telephone companies throughout the United States have a programme called 'phone power' which is offered to employees who use the telephone for selling their services or products. In this programme they suggest that you smile when talking on the phone. Your 'smile' comes through in your voice.

Robert Cryer, manager of a computer department for a Cincinnati, Ohio, company, told how he had successfully found the right applicant for a hard-to-fill position, 'I was desperately trying to recruit a Ph.D. in computer science for my department. I finally located a young man with ideal qualification who was about to be graduated from Purdue University. After several phone conversations I learned that he had several offers from other companies, many of them larger and better known than mine. I was delighted when he accepted my offer. After he started on the job, I asked him why he had chosen us over the others. He paused for a moment and then he said, "I think it was because managers in the other companies spoke on the phone in a cold, business-like manner, which made me feel like just another business transaction. Your voice sounded as if you were glad to hear from me...that you really wanted me to be part of your organisation." You can be assured, I am still answering my phone with a smile.'

The chairman of the board of directors of one of the largest rubber companies in the United States told me that, according to his observations, people rarely succeed at anything unless they have fun doing it. This industrial leader doesn't put much faith in the old adage that hard work alone is the magic key that will unlock the door to our desires. 'I have known people,' he said, 'who succeeded because they had a rip-roaring good time conducting their business. Later, I saw those people change as the fun became work. The business had grown dull. They lost all joy in it, and they failed.'

You must have a good time meeting people if you expect them to have a good time meeting you.

I have asked thousands of business people to smile at someone every hour of the day for a week and then come to class and talk about the results. How did it work? Let's see. Here is a letter from William B. Steinhardt, a New York stockbroker. His case isn't isolated. In fact, it is typical of hundreds of cases.

'I have been married for over eighteen years,' wrote Mr Steinhardt, 'and in all that time I seldom smiled at my wife or spoke two dozen words to her from the time I got up until I was ready to leave for business. I was one of the worst grouches who ever walked down Broadway.

'When you asked me to make a talk about my experience with smiles, I thought I would try it for a week. So the next morning, while combing my hair, I looked at my glum mug in the mirror and said to myself, "Bill, you are going to wipe the scowl off that sour puss of yours today. You are going to smile. And you are going to begin right now." As I sat down to breakfast, I greeted my wife with a "Good morning, my dear," and smiled as I said it.

'You warned me that she might be surprised. Well, you underestimated her reaction. She was bewildered. She was shocked. I told her that in the future she could expect this as a regular occurrence, and I kept it up every morning.

'This changed attitude of mine brought more happiness into our home in the two months since I started than there was during the last year.

'As I leave for my office, I greet the elevator operator in the apartment house with a "Good morning" and a smile. I greet the doorman with a smile. I smile at the cashier in the subway booth when I ask for change. As I stand on the floor of the Stock Exchange, I smile at people who until recently never saw me smile.

'I soon found that everybody was smiling back at me. I treat those who come to me with complaints or grievances in a cheerful manner. I smile as I listen to them and I find that adjustments are accomplished much easier. I find that smiles are bringing me dollars, many dollars every day.

'I share my office with another broker. One of his clerks is a likable young chap, and I was so elated about the results I was getting that I told him recently about my new philosophy of human relations. He then confessed that when I first came to share my office with his firm he thought me a terrible grouch— and only recently changed his mind. He said I was really human when I smiled.

'I have also eliminated criticism from my system. I give appreciation and praise now instead of condemnation. I have stopped talking about what I want. I am now trying to see the other person's viewpoint. And these things have literally revolutionised my life. I am a totally different man, a happier man, a richer man, richer in friendships and happiness—the only things that matter much after all.'

HAPPINESS SHOULDN'T BE AFFECTED BY OUTSIDE FORCES

You don't feel like smiling? Then what? Two things. First, force yourself to smile. If you are alone, force yourself to whistle or hum a tune or sing. Act as if you were already happy, and that will tend to make you happy. Here is the way the psychologist and philosopher William James put it.

'Action seems to follow feeling, but really action and feeling go together; and by regulating the action, which is under the more direct control of the will, we can indirectly regulate the feeling, which is not.

'Thus the sovereign voluntary path to cheerfulness, if our

cheerfulness be lost, is to sit up cheerfully and to act and speak as if cheerfulness were already there...'

Everybody in the world is seeking happiness—and there is one sure way to find it. That is by controlling your thoughts. Happiness doesn't depend on outward conditions. It depends on inner conditions.

It isn't what you have or who you are or where you are or what you are doing that makes you happy or unhappy. It is what you think about it. For example, two people may be in the same place, doing the same thing; both may have about an equal amount of money and prestige—and yet one may be miserable and the other happy. Why? Because of a different mental attitude. I have seen just as many happy faces among the poor peasants toiling with their primitive tools in the devastating heat of the tropics as I have seen in air-conditioned offices in New York, Chicago or Los Angeles.

'There is nothing either good or bad,' said Shakespeare, 'but thinking makes it so.'

Abe Lincoln once remarked that, 'Most folks are about as happy as they make up their minds to be.' He was right. I saw a vivid illustration of that truth as I was walking up the stairs of the Long Island Railroad station in New York. Directly in front of me thirty or forty crippled boys on canes and crutches were struggling up the stairs. One boy had to be carried up. I was astonished at their laughter and gaiety. I spoke about it to one of the men in charge of the boys. 'Oh, yes,' he said, 'when a boy realises that he is going to be a cripple for life, he is shocked at first; but after he gets over the shock, he usually resigns himself to his fate and then becomes as happy as normal boys.'

I felt like taking my hat off to those boys. They taught me a lesson I hope I shall never forget.

Working all by oneself in a closed-off room in an office not only is lonely, but it denies one the opportunity of making friends with other employees in the company. Senora Maria Gonzalez of Guadalajara, Mexico, had such a job. She envied the shared comradeship of other people in the company as she heard their chatter and laughter. As she passed them in the hall during the first weeks of her employment, she shyly looked the other way.

After a few weeks, she said to herself, 'Maria, you can't expect those women to come to you. You have to go out and meet them.' The next time she walked to the water cooler, she put on her brightest smile and said, 'Hi, how are you today' to each of the people she met. The effect was immediate. Smiles and hellos were returned, the hallway seemed brighter, the job friendlier. Acquaintanceships developed and some ripened into friendships. Her job and her life became more pleasant and interesting.

Peruse this bit of sage advice from the essayist and publisher Elbert Hubbard—but remember, perusing it won't do you any good unless you apply it:

> Whenever you go out-of-doors, draw the chin in, carry the crown of the head high and fill the lungs to the utmost; drink in the sunshine; greet your friends with a smile, and put soul into every handclasp. Do not fear being misunderstood and do not waste a minute thinking about your enemies. Try to fix firmly in your mind what you would like to do; and then, without veering off direction, you will move straight to the goal. Keep your mind on the great and splendid things you would like to do, and then, as the days go gliding away, you will find yourself unconsciously seizing upon the

opportunities that are required for the fulfilment of your desire, just as the coral insect takes from the running tide the element it needs. Picture in your mind the able, earnest, useful person you desire to be, and the thought you hold is hourly transforming you into that particular individual... Thought is supreme. Preserve a right mental attitude—the attitude of courage, frankness and good cheer. To think rightly is to create. All things come through desire and every sincere prayer is answered. We become like that on which our hearts are fixed. Carry your chin in and the crown of your head high. We are gods in the chrysalis.

The ancient Chinese were a wise lot—wise in the ways of the world; and they had a proverb that you and I ought to cut out and paste inside our hats. It goes like this, 'A man without a smiling face must not open a shop.'

Your smile is a messenger of your goodwill. Your smile brightens the lives of all who see it. To someone who has seen a dozen people frown, scowl or turn their faces away, your smile is like the sun breaking through the clouds. Especially when that someone is under pressure from his bosses, his customers, his teachers or parents or children, a smile can help him realise that all is not hopeless—that there is joy in the world.

Some years ago, a department store in New York City, in recognition of the pressures its sales clerks were under during the Christmas rush, presented the readers of its advertisements with the following homely philosophy:

THE VALUE OF A SMILE AT CHRISTMAS

It costs nothing, but creates much.

It enriches those who receive, without impoverishing those who give. It happens in a flash and the memory of it sometimes lasts forever. None are so rich they can get along without it, and none so poor but are richer for its benefits.

It creates happiness in the home, fosters goodwill in a business and is the countersign of friends.

It is rest to the weary, daylight to the discouraged, sunshine to the sad and nature's best antidote for trouble.

Yet it cannot be bought, begged, borrowed or stolen, for it is something that is no earthly good to anybody till it is given away.

And if in the last-minute rush of Christmas buying some of our salespeople should be too tired to give you a smile, may we ask you to leave one of yours?

For nobody needs a smile so much as those who have none left to give!

POINTS TO REMEMBER

1. Smile, it doesn't charge you anything.
2. If you think about negative things only, you'll live a miserable life.
3. Your mental attitude determines your success.

12

TEAMING UP FOR TOMORROW

It used to be that big organizations were shaped like pyramids. They had many workers on the bottom and layer after layer of supervisors and middle managers above. Each layer had more authority than the one beneath it. And this multi-layered structure rose ever so neatly to a perfect, predictable point—where the CEO, the chairman and the board of directors got to sit.

Was this the best way to organize a company, a hospital, a school? Almost no one ever bothered to ask. The old pyramid was as it always had been: solid, impressive and seemingly impervious to change.

Now this might come as a surprise to some people, but the pyramids are tumbling down. It's as if the slaves of ancient Egypt decided to return and they're carting away the stones. The new landscape may never be as flat as the sandy Sahara. But you can bet the future will be a whole lot more horizontal than the past.

All those rigid hierarchies, all those departmental lines, all those intricate chains of command—all of it stifled creative work. And who can afford that when the world is changing so fast?

'Look at what happened to the former USSR as a

hierarchy,' says Richard C. Bartlett, vice chairman of Mary Kay Corporation. 'The same thing will probably happen to China because of hierarchy. It doesn't work for governments. It doesn't work for corporations either. The biggest corporations we've got in the United States didn't even notice the world coming down around their ears.'

Clearly what's been needed is a structure that loosens up the old rigidity, that could let people do their creative best, that could fully develop the talent that's been lying dormant for years. In more and more well-led organizations, the answer is being found in teams. Increasingly often, people are being asked to work beyond their disciplines, outside their cultures, above and below their usual ranks.

'The modern organization cannot be an organization of boss and subordinate,' argues business theorist Peter Drucker, professor of management at the Claremont Graduate School in California. 'It must be organized as a team.'

Andrés Navarro, president of Chile's SONDA, S.A., agrees. 'The Lone Ranger is no longer possible,' Navarro observes. 'A guy by himself inventing something alone—the world is too complicated for that. You need several people from different disciplines working together at the same time.'

Small groups of people, recruited from throughout the organization, brought together for ongoing projects or for some specific, limited task—to design a new product, to reorganize a plant, to restructure a department, to figure out how to add momentum to a quality-improvement program. Fading are the old departmental rivalries. And fading are the automatic promotions, the seniority-based pay scales and the other frustrating vestiges of the old pyramid.

In pyramid companies, the engineers spent all day cooped up with other engineers. Now an engineer might just as easily be thrown into a group of salespeople and told, 'Help make this product more attractive to the customer.' Or 'Figure out how to build that part faster.' Or 'Use your engineering expertise to guide this marketing group around a technical glitch.'

As a result of groupings like this, marketing is actually listening to engineering, and engineering is listening back. At many big companies this never, ever happened before. And now manufacturing, customer service, labour relations and all the other far-flung departments are communicating too. At some progressive companies, these entire artificial divisions are even beginning to disappear.

As Drucker argues, the world is not made up of privates and drill sergeants anymore. 'The army was organized by command-and-control, and business enterprise as well as most other institutions copied that model,' he writes. 'This is now rapidly changing. As more and more organizations become information-based, they are transforming themselves into soccer or tennis teams—that is, into responsibility-based organizations in which every member must act as a responsible decision-maker. All members have to see themselves as executives.'

Look at how the Mary Kay Corporation is organized. 'The Mary Kay organizational structure is a free form,' says Vice Chairman Richard Bartlett. 'I like to think of it almost as a molecular structure, where people can go right through any artificial barriers. They are not confined to a box. They can participate in a creative action team right across departmental lines. And in our view of the world—and this sounds trite to say, but a few people have jumped on the bandwagon since—the customer is right smack on top.

'But in the way we do business, right below her is our sales force. Our organization is very focused on how to support that sales force. At the bottom of the organizational chart is something that is referred to as an insignificant green dot.

'The first time I ever did a slide presentation on how to structure an organization, the artist put a green dot down there,' Bartlett recalls. 'I'm the insignificant green dot. My personal view of the world is that there is no need for a president or chairman unless he is dedicated to serving the needs of others and to providing resources to the people who are getting the job done.'

'Organizations are actually restructuring,' says Adele Scheele, whose articles on career-management issues appear regularly in American and Japanese business magazines. 'What used to work no longer works. People expected there would be a set path, and there is no set path. So the more you believe in that, the less likely you are to be able to be flexible and begin to take advantage of opportunities that never come labelled. You want to always be open.'

These flattened organizations are turning up in all kinds of surprising places, even in the educational world. 'Management is becoming a lot flatter,' observes Marc Horowitz, principal of Cantiague Elementary School in Jericho, New York. 'And there's a real need to build teams, lead teams and motivate people horizontally. In many cases it has to be done without title, without financial remuneration or incentive. It's the team's performance that's key.'

What this means in Horowitz's school is that students no longer work by themselves all day long in rows of wooden desks. They cooperate. They work in teams. They produce group projects. The students are expected to help each other. The teachers also work more cooperatively than they ever have before. 'Now it's "How do we relate together and get results in the real world?"' Horowitz explains. 'We're preparing students for the future. They really can't work in isolation anymore. They have to get involved in a team effort, and half of that battle is learning the social skills to encourage those in the group who aren't doing so well. They should never be allowed to feel less than worthy because they slip up or they do not have all the answers.'

Three first-graders at Horowitz's school were involved in a group project one day. One of the children had the task of writing the word two on a piece of paper. But the child misspelled the word, writing it as tow. When a girl in the group pointed out the error, the boy felt bad for a moment. But then the little girl said, 'Don't worry about it. I know you misspelled it. But that was a beautiful w, okay?' She even gave him a pat on the knee, and all three of the students got a good lesson in working cooperatively.

The Harvard Business School marketing faculty recently conducted a teamwork experiment with the first-year graduate students. Instead of the usual midterm case-study exam, these students were divided at random into teams of four. Each team was given a business problem to solve—and twenty-four hours to come back with a written plan. The members of each team would get the same grade.

'Initially there was much criticism,' says John Quelch, the Harvard Business School professor. 'Some students complained that individual grades would be adversely affected by the fact that they were thrown into a team with a group of people they wouldn't have selected to work with.' The school's answer: welcome to the real world.

In the end, the Harvard students came around. When the student newspaper surveyed the students after the experience, they expressed an overwhelming support for the new group-project midterm exam.

'The most significant level of learning,' Quelch says, 'was

probably among students in those groups that did not perform like clockwork. There were some groups which experienced tremendous disagreements, and in retrospect, those were the students who learned the most out of the whole process.'

Effective teamwork doesn't happen by magic. It takes a cooperative group of players, and it takes a talented coach. You can't simply throw a few individuals together—even a few highly talented individuals—and expect them to perform brilliantly.

That's why the National Basketball Association all-star game so often falls short of its hype. Sure, the game features many of the finest players in America, brought together on a single basketball court. Pound for pound, there is no more talented collection of guards, forwards and centres anywhere. So why does this floor full of phenomenal talent so seldom produce a phenomenal game?

Too much ego. Too much time in the spotlight. Too many mornings on the sports page. When it comes to playing as part of a unit, these superstars often fail to measure up. The missing ingredient is teamwork.

There is an art to building successful teams, and even a great coach can rarely mould a winner overnight. But anyone who expects to be a leader in the years to come had better master a few basic coaching techniques. They are as necessary in the business world as they are on the basketball court.

CREATE A SHARED SENSE OF PURPOSE

People working together can accomplish tremendous things.

What gives a team that special boost is the unified vision the individual members share.

The ideas, the creativity, the intelligent sparks will ultimately have to come from the group itself. But a strong leader is often needed to focus all that energy—to clarify the vision, to establish goals, to help everyone understand what the team is about, to show the team members how their accomplishments will impact upon the outside world.

Ray Stata, chairman of Analog Devices Inc., says, 'You've got to provide the environment, the corporate objective and the encouragement so that people as individuals and as teams of individuals can feel that they're world-class, that they are better than any other team and that there's recognition and feedback which acknowledges that.'

MAKE THE GOALS TEAM-GOALS

Unless the whole team wins, no one wins. This concept is most familiar in the world of sports, but it's just as true for teams of any sort. Individual records are fine for the history books, but really they're an afterthought. What matters far more is the performance of the entire team.

'When you get people involved in this way and they feed off each other, it's contagious,' says Rubbermaid's Wolfgang Schmitt. 'It becomes a lot more like being a member of a sports team versus being in an assembly line. There's just a big difference in the energy level they bring into the work, the intensity.'

That's why most good coaches—and most good leaders—speak so often in the first-person plural. 'We need...' 'Our deadline...' 'The job before us...' Good leaders always emphasize how everyone's contribution fits in.

In business, 'Together we have to get this new product smoothly to market.' If the ad man does marvellous work but the packaging specialist fails, that's not success.

In sailing, 'Together we have to get this boat through the storm.' If the navigator can read the stars like a paperback novel but the skipper doesn't know the difference between starboard and port, that's not success.

In politics, 'Together we have to win this election.' If the candidate is a splendid orator but the advance staff can't get her to the speech, that's not success.

TREAT PEOPLE LIKE THE INDIVIDUALS THEY ARE

When individuals come together as a team, their individuality doesn't suddenly evaporate. They still have different personalities. They still have different skills. They still have different hopes and fears. A talented leader will recognize those differences, appreciate them, and use them to the advantage of the team.

Individually—that's how Bela Karolyi, the internationally renowned gymnastics coach, prepared his students for the Olympic Games. 'If I wasn't producing what he wanted,' recalls Olympic gold medallist Mary Lou Retton, a star student of Karolyi's, 'he would ignore me. I'd rather him yell at me, I swear.' But Karolyi was smart enough to recognize that that approach was exactly what Retton needed.

'I would do a vault,' she recalls. 'I'd put my hands up, and then I'd turn around. He would be looking down at the next girl, who was ready to go. Oh, I wanted his attention so much. I wanted him to say, "That was good, Mary Lou." He would use that to get results out of me, and that would push me to make the correction, to get that praise.'

Was Karolyi just a grouch? Not at all. With other students he took an entirely different tack. Retton will never forget the approach Karolyi used on teammate Julianne McNamara. 'She has a much different personality than I do,' Retton says. 'She's much more timid, a little reserved. He would be very gentle with her. If she wasn't making that correction, he'd come and put her body where it needed to be and talk quietly to her. He was always much more gentle with her. That's how he got personal results.'

'He treated each student differently, and I think that's very important.'

MAKE EACH MEMBER RESPONSIBLE FOR THE TEAM PRODUCT

People need to feel their contributions are important. Otherwise, they'll devote less than complete attention to the tasks at hand.

Make the project belong to the team. Let as many decisions as possible bubble up from the group. Invite participation. Don't dictate solutions. Don't insist that things be done a certain way.

The Jaycraft Corporation had a problem. Its biggest customer had a giant order—and a delivery date that seemed impossible to meet. Doug Van Vechten, the company president, could have imposed a solution from the top.

But he knew better than to try. Instead, he asked a team of his employees to figure out what to do. 'They came back to me and said, "We can move some things around here and there, and we feel that we can do it, and let's take the job,"' Van Vechten remembers. Jaycraft took the job and met the customer's delivery demand.

SHARE THE GLORY, ACCEPT THE BLAME

When the team does well and is recognized, it's the leader's responsibility to spread the benefits around. A public pat on the back, a bonus from the top, a write-up in the company magazine—whatever form that recognition takes, everyone should get a generous share of it.

Denis Potvin, former captain of the New York Islanders hockey team, knew how to share the glory when his team won the Stanley Cup. But just in case he didn't, coach Al Arbour knew enough about team play to remind him. 'Make sure you let the other guys carry the cup,' the coach whispered into Potvin's ear, a few seconds after the final buzzer of the championship game.

'He came on the ice and rushed over to the pile' of celebrating Islanders, Potvin explains. 'We're all congratulating each other. I turned, and Al was there. We both hugged one another. And it was there, in my ear, that he told me that.

'I was very impressed,' Potvin recalls. 'Here is a guy who is in total control of the team. He was still thinking about his players even though the Stanley Cup had just been won—his first time as a coach.'

People always appreciate being included in praise. It encourages them to give their greatest efforts and makes them want to work again with the leader who guided them to this success. And this kind of graciousness has one other benefit: in the end the leader gets a big share of the credit anyway.

When it comes to criticism, be a smart leader and take exactly the opposite approach. Don't point the finger at others. Never raise public complaints about the 'weak link' in the chain. Step forward and accept whatever complaints arrive. Then speak privately with the team members about how the results might be improved, and turn their attention to doing better next time.

TAKE EVERY OPPORTUNITY TO BUILD CONFIDENCE ON THE TEAM

A great leader will believe firmly in the team and will share that belief with every member.

That's a lesson kindergarten teacher Barbara Hammerman puts into action in her classroom, and it applies just as well in the factory or boardroom. 'I try to build a class spirit within the room,' she says. 'To the children in my class, we are the best class, and there is a feeling that we don't want to disappoint the group—one for all and all for one—that we have certain standards that are set and reviewed and continuously reinforced through the year. The children understand these standards.'

They aren't intimidated by them. 'They just love living up to these standards because we're great,' Hammerman said. 'Who doesn't want to feel as if they're part of the wonderful group? When they get compliments from others, they can begin to see the progress they are making and changes in themselves. And they just feel wonderful about themselves.'

BE INVOLVED, STAY INVOLVED

In those old pyramid companies, it was easy for the boss to remain relatively aloof. After all, that army of minions was always hovering around, just waiting to distribute the boss's latest wisdom to the troops.

This approach doesn't fly in the new team-based world. The strong leader has to be involved and stay involved. Visualize the leader as the commander of a busy aircraft carrier, standing out on deck. Planes are coming in. Others are taking off. The ship has to stay on course and also be protected from attack. All these considerations have to be factored in together.

The leader really does have to *be there*. 'You've got to have the experience, and you've got to listen,' says Jack Gallagher, president of North Shore University Hospital in Manhasset, New York. 'But after a while, if you get enough experience, if you work hard enough, if you're smart enough, if you do your homework, then you get a good feel for all these planes going up and down and for all the other things around you.'

You can't always draw up a precise battle plan.

'You've got to get an intuitive feel for it, and you've got to have antennae out, the antennae in the back of your head,' Gallagher says. 'Sure, there are too many things going on, and this is a very complex business. But you can develop that intuitive feel.'

BE A MENTOR

It's the leader's job to develop the talents and strengthen the people on the team. This is true in the short term, as the team members deal with their assignment at hand. But it's also true long-term: the leaders must take a genuine responsibility for the lives and careers of the members of the team.

'How would you like to improve?' 'Where do you want your career to go from here?' 'What kinds of new responsibilities would you like to be taking on?' It's your job as leader to ask all those questions and to use whatever knowledge and experience you possess to help team members achieve those goals.

Reinforce the confidence you have in their abilities. Give them standards to live up to. Issue genuine compliments in public, 'Sally has done a terrific job on this report.' Send private notes, 'That was a great comment you made today. You got us all focused where we needed to be.' And remember, if they succeed, you succeed.

At Harvard University's Graduate School of Business Administration, new faculty members aren't just left to sink or swim.

'All seven or eight instructors teaching our introductory marketing course meet every week for four hours as a group to discuss the cases that are coming up and how best to teach those cases,' says Professor John Quelch. 'They also review how the cases went the previous week, what improvements need to be made and so forth. In this way, newly recruited instructors can pick up teaching tips from our more experienced faculty.'

The senior faculty members also provide other kinds of support. Three or four times a semester, one of them sits in on a new instructor's class. They come to help, not to judge. 'They're there very much in a coaching role,' Quelch explains, 'rather than to develop a report for a file that's going to determine your promotion. The goal is to enhance the effectiveness of the asset—the new faculty member—that we've invested in.'

After class the senior faculty member might provide advice for both short- and long-term improvement. 'What I would try to say to a new faculty member,' Quelch continues, 'is, "Here are five things you can do the next time you teach that will have a positive impact on the way you're received by the class." Suggestions might include, for example, something as seemingly trivial as writing larger on the blackboard. Or "Make sure that you don't hang around the blackboard and direct the class from one area at the front of the room. Wander around the entire room and stand behind the students. Share the experience."'

As Walter Lippmann wrote upon the death of Franklin Delano Roosevelt, 'The final test of a leader is that he leaves behind him in other men the conviction and the will to carry on.'

Follow these few simple techniques and watch how your team succeeds. The greatest reward a leader can achieve—the greatest legacy a leader can leave—is a group of talented, self-confident and cooperative people, who are themselves ready to lead.

POINTS TO REMEMBER

1. Hollowness of the pyramid structure of an organisation.
2. Modern workplace can't be a place of boss and subordinate. But of a team.
3. A team's special boost is the unified vision the individual members share.

13

HOW TO ENCOURAGE PEOPLE

Pete Barlow was an old friend of mine. He had a dog-and-pony act and spent his life travelling with circuses and vaudeville shows. I loved to watch Pete train new dogs for his act. I noticed that the moment a dog showed the slightest improvement, Pete patted and praised him and gave him meat and made a great to do about it.

That's nothing new. Animal trainers have been using that same technique for centuries.

Why, I wonder, don't we use the same common sense when trying to change people that we use when trying to change dogs? Why don't we use meat instead of a whip? Why don't we use praise instead of condemnation? Let us praise even the slightest improvement. That inspires the other person to keep on improving.

I can look back at my own life and see where a few words of praise have sharply changed my entire future. Can't you say the same thing about your life? History is replete with striking illustrations of the sheer witchery of praise.

For example, many years ago a boy of ten was working in a factory in Naples. He longed to be a singer, but his first teacher discouraged him. 'You can't sing,' he said. 'You haven't any voice at all. It sounds like the wind in the shutters.'

But his mother, a poor peasant woman, put her arms about him and praised him and told him she knew he could sing, she could already see an improvement, and she went barefoot in order to save money to pay for his music lessons. That peasant mother's praise and encouragement changed that boy's life. His name was Enrico Caruso, and he became the greatest and most famous opera singer of his age.

In the early 19th century, a young man in London aspired to be a writer. But everything seemed to be against him. He had never been able to attend school more than four years. His father had been flung in jail because he couldn't pay his debts, and this young man often knew the pangs of hunger. Finally, he got a job pasting labels on bottles of blacking in a rat-infested warehouse, and he slept at night in a dismal attic room with two other boys—guttersnipes from the slums of London. He had so little confidence in his ability to write that he sneaked out and mailed his first manuscript in the dead of night so nobody would laugh at him. Story after story was refused. Finally, the great day came when one was accepted. True, he wasn't paid a shilling for it, but one editor had praised him. One editor had given him recognition. He was so thrilled that he wandered aimlessly around the streets with tears rolling down his cheeks.

The praise, the recognition, that he received through getting one story in print, changed his whole life, for if it hadn't been for that encouragement, he might have spent his entire life working in rat-infested factories. You may have heard of that boy. His name was Charles Dickens.

Another boy in London made his living as a clerk in a dry-goods store. He had to get up at 5 a.m., sweep out the store and slave for fourteen hours a day. It was sheer drudgery and he despised it. After two years, he could stand it no longer, so he got up one morning and, without waiting for breakfast, tramped fifteen miles to talk to his mother, who was working as a housekeeper.

He was frantic. He pleaded with her. He wept. He swore he would kill himself if he had to remain in the shop any longer. Then he wrote a long, pathetic letter to his old schoolmaster, declaring that he was heartbroken, that he no longer wanted to live. His old schoolmaster gave him a little praise and assured him that he really was very intelligent and fitted for finer things and offered him a job as a teacher.

That praise changed the future of that boy and made a lasting impression on the history of English literature. For that boy went on to write innumerable best-selling books and made over a million dollars with his pen. You've probably heard of him. His name: H. G. Wells.

Use of praise instead of criticism is the basic concept of B. F. Skinner's teachings. This great contemporary psychologist has shown by experiments with animals and with humans that when criticism is minimised and praise emphasised, the good things people do will be reinforced and the poorer things will atrophy for lack of attention.

Everybody likes to be praised, but when praise is specific, it comes across as sincere—not something the other person may be saying just to make one feel good.

Remember, we all crave appreciation and recognition, and will do almost anything to get it. But nobody wants insincerity. Nobody wants flattery.

Let me repeat: the principles taught in this book will work only when they come from the heart. I am not advocating a bag of tricks. I am talking about a new way of life.

Talking about changing people. If you and I will inspire the people with whom we come in contact to a realisation of the hidden treasures they possess, we can do far more than change people. We can literally transform them.

Exaggeration? Then listen to these sage words from William James, one of the most distinguished psychologists and philosophers America has ever produced:

> Compared with what we ought to be, we are only half awake. We are making use of only a small part of our physical and mental resources. Stating the thing broadly, the human individual thus lives far within his limits. He possesses powers of various sorts which he habitually fails to use.

Yes, you who are reading these lines possess powers of various sorts which you habitually fail to use; and one of these powers you are probably not using to the fullest extent is your magic ability to praise people and inspire them with a realisation of their latent possibilities.

POINTS TO REMEMBER

1. Praising someone can act as a good motivator for them.
2. Usage of praise instead of criticism for improvement.
3. Difference between praise and flattery.

14

A LAW THAT WILL OUTLAW MANY OF YOUR WORRIES

As a child, I grew up on a Missouri farm; and one day, while helping my mother pit cherries, I began to cry. My mother said, 'Dale, what in the world are you crying about?' I blubbered, 'I'm afraid I am going to be buried alive!'

I was full of worries in those days. When thunderstorms came, I worried for fear I would be killed by lightning. When hard times came, I worried for fear we wouldn't have enough to eat. I worried for fear I would go to hell when I died. I was terrified for fear an older boy, Sam White, would cut off my big ears—as he threatened to do. I worried for fear girls would laugh at me if I tipped my hat to them. I worried for fear no girl would ever be willing to marry me. I worried about what I would say to my wife immediately after we were married. I imagined that we would be married in some country church, and then get in a surrey with fringe on the top and ride back to the farm…but how would I be able to keep the conversation going on that ride back to the farm? How? How? I pondered over that earth-shaking problem for many an hour as I walked behind the plough.

As the years went by, I gradually discovered that ninety-nine per cent of the things I worried about never happened.

For example, as I have already said, I was once terrified of lightning; but I now know that the chances of my being killed by lightning in any one year are, according to the National Safety Council, only one in three hundred and fifty thousand.

My fear of being buried alive was even more absurd: I don't imagine that—even back in the days before embalming was the rule—that one person in ten million was buried alive; yet I once cried for fear of it.

One person out of every eight dies of cancer. If I had wanted something to worry about, I should have worried about cancer—instead of being killed by lightning or being buried alive.

To be sure, I have been talking about the worries of youth and adolescence. But many of our adult worries are almost as absurd. You and I could probably eliminate nine tenths of our worries right now if we would cease our fretting long enough to discover whether, *by the law of averages,* there was any real justification for our worries.

THE LAW OF AVERAGES

The most famous insurance company on earth—Lloyd's of London—has made countless millions of dollars out of the tendency of everybody to worry about things that rarely happen. Lloyd's of London bets people that the disasters they are worrying about will never occur. However, *they don't call it betting. They call it insurance. But it is really betting based on the law of averages.* This great insurance firm has been going strong for two hundred years; and unless human nature changes, it will still be going strong fifty centuries from now by insuring shoes and ships and sealing wax against disasters that, *by the law of averages,* don't happen nearly so often as people imagine.

General George Crook—probably the greatest Indian fighter in American history—says on page 77 of his *Autobiography* that, 'nearly all the worries and unhappiness' of the Indians 'came from their imagination, and not from reality.'

As I look back across the decades, I can see that that is where most of my worries came from also. Jim Grant told me that that had been his experience, too. He owns the James A. Grant Distributing Company, 204 Franklin Street, New York City. He orders from ten to fifteen carloads of Florida oranges and grapefruit at a time. He told me that he used to torture himself with such thoughts as: what if there's a train wreck? What if my fruit is strewn all over the countryside? What if a bridge collapses as my cars are going across it? Of course, the fruit was insured; but he feared that if he didn't deliver his fruit on time, he might risk the loss of his market. He worried so much that he feared he had stomach ulcers and went to a doctor. The doctor told him there was nothing wrong with him except jumpy nerves. 'I saw the light then,' he said, 'and began to ask myself questions. I said to myself, "Look here, Jim Grant, how many fruit cars have you handled over the years?" The answer was, "About twenty-five thousand." Then I asked myself, "How many of those cars were ever wrecked?" The answer was, "Oh—maybe five." Then I said to myself, "Only five—out of twenty-five thousand? Do you know what that means? A ratio of five thousand to one! In other words, by the law of averages, based on experience, the chances are five thousand to one against one of your cars ever being wrecked. So what are you worried about?"

'Then I said to myself, "Well, a bridge may collapse!" Then I asked myself, "How many cars have you actually lost from a bridge collapsing?" The answer was—"None." Then I said to myself, "Aren't you a fool to be worrying yourself into stomach ulcers over a bridge which has never yet collapsed, and over a railroad wreck when the chances are five thousand to one against it!"

'When I looked at it that way,' Jim Grant told me, 'I felt pretty silly. I decided then and there to let the law of averages do the worrying for me—and I have not been troubled with my "stomach ulcer" since!'

When Al Smith was Governor of New York, I heard him answer the attacks of his political enemies by saying over and over, 'Let's examine the record ... let's examine the record.' Then he proceeded to give the facts. The next time you and I are worrying about what may happen, let's take a tip from wise old Al Smith: let's examine the record and see what basis there is, if any, for our gnawing anxieties. That is precisely what Frederick J. Mahlstedt did when he feared he was lying in his grave. Here is his story as he told it to one of our adult-education classes in New York:

'Early in June, 1944, I was lying in a slit trench near Omaha Beach. I was with the 999th Signal Service Company, and we had just "dug in" in Normandy. As I looked around at that slit trench—just a rectangular hole in the ground—I said to myself, "This looks just like a grave." When I lay down and tried to sleep in it, it felt like a grave. I couldn't help saying to myself, *"Maybe this is my grave."* When the German bombers began coming over at 11 **p.m.,** and the bombs started falling, I was scared stiff. For the first two or three nights I couldn't sleep at all. By the fourth or fifth night, I was almost a nervous wreck. I knew that if I didn't do something, I would go stark crazy. So I reminded myself that five nights had passed, and I was still alive; and so was every man in our outfit. Only two had even been injured, and they had been hurt, not by German bombs, but by falling flak, from our own antiaircraft guns.

'I decided to stop worrying by doing something constructive. So I built a thick wooden roof over my slit trench, to protect myself from flak. I thought of the vast area over which my unit was spread. I told myself that the only way I could be killed in that deep, narrow slit trench was by a direct hit; and I figured out that the chance of a direct hit on me was not one in ten thousand. After a couple of nights of looking at it in this way, I calmed down and slept even through the bomb raids!'

POINTS TO REMEMBER

1. Ninety-nine per cent of the things we worry about never happen.
2. Let the law of averages do the worrying for you.
3. Instead of worrying, spend your time doing something productive.

15

RIGHT THINKING AND PERSONALITY

The speaker's most valuable possession is personality—that indefinable, imponderable something which sums up what we are, and makes us different from others; that distinctive force of self which operates appreciably on those whose lives we touch. It is personality alone that makes us long for higher things. Rob us of our sense of individual life, with its gains and losses, its duties and joys and we grovel. Says John Stuart Mill,

> *Few human creatures, 'would consent to be changed into any of the lower animals for a promise of the fullest allowance of a beast's pleasures; no intelligent human being would consent to be a fool, no instructed person would be an ignoramus, no person of feeling and conscience would be selfish and base, even though he should be persuaded that the fool, or the dunce, or the rascal is better satisfied with his lot than they with theirs... It is better to be a human being dissatisfied than a pig satisfied, better to be a Socrates dissatisfied than a fool satisfied. And if the fool or the pig is of a different opinion, it is only because they know only their own side of the question. The other party to the comparison knows both sides.'*

Now it is precisely because the Socrates-type of person lives on the plane of right thinking and restrained feeling and willing, that he prefers his state to that of the animal. All that a man is, all his happiness, his sorrow, his achievements, his failures, his magnetism, his weakness, all are in an amazingly large measure the direct results of his thinking. Thought and heart combine to produce right thinking: 'As a man thinketh in his heart so is he.' As he does not think in his heart so he can never become.

Since this is true, personality can be developed and its latent powers brought out by careful cultivation. We have long since ceased to believe that we are living in a realm of chance. So clear and exact are nature's laws that we forecast, scores of years in advance, the appearance of a certain comet and foretell to the minute an eclipse of the sun. And we understand this law of cause and effect in all our material realms. We do not plant potatoes and expect to pluck hyacinths. The law is universal: it applies to our mental powers, to morality, to personality, quite as much as to the heavenly bodies and the grain of the fields. 'Whatsoever a man soweth that shall he also reap,' and nothing else.

Character has always been regarded as one of the chief factors of the speaker's power. Cato defined the orator as *vir bonus dicendi peritus*—a good man skilled in speaking. Phillips Brooks says, 'Nobody can truly stand as a utterer before the world, unless he be profoundly living and earnestly thinking.' Emerson says:

> *Character is a natural power like light and heat, and all nature cooperates with it. The reason why we feel one man's presence, and do not feel another's is as simple as gravity. Truth is the summit of being: justice is the application of it to affairs. All individual natures stand in a scale, according to the purity of this element in them. The will of the pure runs down into other natures, as water runs down from a*

higher into a lower vessel. This natural force is no more to be withstood than any other natural force... Character is nature in the highest form.'

WATER YOUR MIND

It is absolutely impossible for impure, bestial and selfish thoughts to blossom into loving and altruistic habits. Thistle seeds bring forth only the thistle. Contrariwise, it is entirely impossible for continual altruistic, sympathetic and serviceful thoughts to bring forth a low and vicious character. Either thoughts or feelings precede and determine all our actions. Actions develop into habits, habits constitute character and character determines destiny. Therefore, to guard our thoughts and control our feelings is to shape our destinies. The syllogism is complete, and old as it is it is, still true.

Since 'character is nature in the highest form,' the development of character must proceed on natural lines. The garden left to itself will bring forth weeds and scrawny plants, but the flower-beds nurtured carefully will blossom into fragrance and beauty.

As the student entering college largely determines his vocation by choosing from the different courses of the curriculum, so do we choose our characters by choosing our thoughts. We are steadily going up toward that which we most wish for, or steadily sinking to the level of our low desires. What we secretly cherish in our hearts is a symbol of what we shall receive. Our trains of thoughts are hurrying us on to our destiny. When you see the flag fluttering to the South, you know the wind is coming from the North. When you see the straws and papers being carried to the Northward you realize the wind is blowing out of the South. It is just as easy to ascertain a man's thoughts by observing the tendency of his character.

Let it not be suspected for one moment that all this is merely a preachment on the question of morals. It is that, but much more, for it touches the whole man—his imaginative nature, his ability to control his feelings, the mastery of his thinking faculties, and—perhaps most largely—his power to will and to carry his volitions into effective action.

Right thinking constantly assumes that the will sits enthroned to execute the dictates of mind, conscience and heart. Never tolerate for an instant the suggestion that your will is not absolutely efficient. The way to will is to will—and the very first time you are tempted to break a worthy resolution—and you will be, you may be certain of that—make your fight then and there. You cannot afford to lose that fight. You must win it—don't swerve for an instant, but keep that resolution if it kills you. It will not, but you must fight just as though life depended on the victory; and indeed, your personality may actually lie in the balances!

Your success or failure as a speaker will be determined very largely by your thoughts and your mental attitude. The present writer had a student of limited education enter one of his classes in public speaking. He proved to be a very poor speaker; and the instructor could conscientiously do little but point out faults. However, the young man was warned not to be discouraged. With sorrow in his voice and the essence of earnestness beaming from his eyes, he replied, 'I will not be discouraged! I want so badly to know how to speak!' It was warm, human and from the very heart. And he did keep on trying—and developed into a creditable speaker.

There is no power under the stars that can defeat a man with that attitude. He who down in the deeps of his heart earnestly longs to get facility in speaking, and is willing to make the sacrifices necessary, will reach his goal. 'Ask and ye shall receive; seek and ye shall find; knock and it shall be opened unto you,' is indeed applicable to those who would acquire speech-power. You will not realize the prize that you wish for languidly, but the goal that you start out to attain with the spirit of the old guard that dies but never surrenders, you will surely reach.

Your belief in your ability and your willingness to make sacrifices for that belief, are the double index to your future achievements. Lincoln had a dream of his possibilities as a speaker. He transmuted that dream into life solely because he walked many miles to borrow books which he read by the log-fire glow at night. He sacrificed much to realize his vision. Livingstone had a great faith in his ability to serve the benighted races of Africa. To actualize that faith he gave up all. Leaving England for the interior of the Dark Continent he struck the death blow to Europe's profits from the slave trade. Joan of Arc had great self-confidence, glorified by an infinite capacity for sacrifice. She drove the English beyond the Loire and stood beside Charles while he was crowned.

These all realized their strongest desires. The law is universal. Desire greatly, and you shall achieve; sacrifice much, and you shall obtain.

Stanton Davis Kirkham has beautifully expressed this thought:

> *You may be keeping accounts, and presently you shall walk out of the door that has for so long seemed to you the barrier of your ideals, and shall find yourself before an audience—the pen still behind your ear, the ink stains on your fingers—and then and there shall pour out the torrent of your inspiration. You may be driving sheep, and you shall wander to the city—*

bucolic and open-mouthed; shall wander under the intrepid guidance of the spirit into the studio of the master, and after a time he shall say, 'I have nothing more to teach you.' And now you have become the master, who did so recently dream of great things while driving sheep. You shall lay down the saw and the plane to take upon yourself the regeneration of the world.

POINTS TO REMEMBER

1. It is your personality that makes you a leader and not a follower, so nurture it.
2. Right thinking and strong will are required to abstain from temptations.
3. You cannot obtain anything without sacrificing something.

16

HOW TO CRITICIZE—AND NOT BE HATED FOR IT

Charles Schwab was passing through one of his steel mills one day at noon when he came across some of his employees smoking. Immediately above their heads was a sign that said No Smoking. Did Schwab point to the sign and say, 'Can't you read?' Oh, no, not Schwab. He walked over to the men, handed each one a cigar, and said, 'I'll appreciate it, boys, if you will smoke these on the outside.' They knew that he knew that they had broken a rule—and they admired him because he said nothing about it and gave them a little present and made them feel important. Couldn't keep from loving a man like that, could you?

John Wanamaker used the same technique. Wanamaker used to make a tour of his great store in Philadelphia every day. Once he saw a customer waiting at a counter. No one was paying the slightest attention to her. The salespeople? Oh, they were in a huddle at the far end of the counter laughing and talking among themselves. Wanamaker didn't say a word. Quietly slipping behind the counter, he waited on the woman himself and then handed the purchase to the salespeople to be wrapped as he went on his way.

Public officials are often criticized for not being accessible to their constituents. They are busy people, and the fault sometimes lies in overprotective assistants who don't want to overburden their bosses with too many visitors. Carl Langford, who had been mayor of Orlando, Florida, the home of Disney World, for many years, frequently admonished his staff to allow people to see him. He claimed he had an 'open-door' policy; yet the citizens of his community were blocked by secretaries and administrators when they called.

Finally, the mayor found the solution. He removed the door from his office! His aides got the message, and the mayor had a truly open administration from the day his door was symbolically thrown away.

Simply changing one three-letter word can often spell the difference between failure and success in changing people without giving offense or arousing resentment.

Many people begin their criticism with sincere praise followed by the word 'but' and ending with a critical statement. For example, in trying to change a child's careless attitude toward studies, we might say, 'We're really proud of you, Johnnie, for raising your grades this term. *But* if you had worked harder on your algebra, the results would have been better.'

In this case, Johnnie might feel encouraged until he heard the word 'but'. He might then question the sincerity of the original praise. To him, the praise might seem only to be a contrived lead-in to a critical inference of failure. Credibility would be strained, and we probably would not achieve our objective of changing Johnnie's attitude toward his studies.

This could be easily overcome by changing the word 'but' to 'and'. 'We're really proud of you, Johnnie, for raising your grades this term, *and* if you continue the same conscientious efforts next term, your algebra grade can be up with all the others.'

Now, Johnnie would accept the praise because there was no follow-up of an inference of failure. We have called his attention to the behaviour we wished to change indirectly and the chances are he will try to live up to our expectations.

Calling attention indirectly to someone's mistakes works wonders with sensitive people who may resent bitterly any direct criticism. Marge Jacob of Woonsocket, Rhode Island, told one of our classes how she convinced some sloppy construction workers to clean up after themselves when they were building additions to her house.

For the first few days of the work, when Mrs. Jacob returned from her job, she noticed that the yard was strewn with the cut ends of lumber. She didn't want to antagonize the builders, because they did excellent work. So after the workers had gone home, she and her children picked up and neatly piled all the lumber debris in a corner. The following morning she called the foreman to one side and said, 'I'm really pleased with the way the front lawn was left last night; it is nice and clean and does not offend the neighbours.' From that day forward the workers picked up and piled the debris to one side, and the foreman came in each day seeking approval of the condition the lawn was left in after a day's work.

One of the major areas of controversy between members of the army reserves and their regular army trainers is haircuts. The reservists consider themselves civilians (which they are most of the time) and resent having to cut their hair short.

Master Sergeant Harley Kaiser of the 542nd USAR School addressed himself to this problem when he was working with a group of reserve non-commissioned officers. As an old-time regular-army master sergeant, he might have been expected to yell at his troops and threaten them. Instead he chose to make his point indirectly.

'Gentlemen,' he started, 'you are leaders. You will be most effective when you lead by example. You must be the example for your men to follow. You know what the army regulations say about haircuts. I am going to get my hair cut today, although it is still much shorter than some of yours. You look at yourself in the mirror, and if you feel you need a haircut to be a good example, we'll arrange time for you to visit the post barbershop.'

The result was predictable. Several of the candidates did look in the mirror and went to the barbershop that afternoon and received 'regulation' haircuts. Sergeant Kaiser commented the next morning that he already could see the development of leadership qualities in some of the members of the squad.

On March 8, 1887, the eloquent Henry Ward Beecher died. The following Sunday, Lyman Abbott was invited to speak in the pulpit left silent by Beecher's passing. Eager to do his best, he wrote, rewrote and polished his sermon with the meticulous care of a Flaubert. Then he read it to his wife. It was poor—as most written speeches are. She might have said, if she had had less judgment, 'Lyman, that is terrible. That'll never do. You'll put people to sleep. It reads like an encyclopaedia. You ought to know better than that after all the years you have been preaching. For heaven's sake, why don't you talk like a human being? Why don't you act natural? You'll disgrace yourself if you ever read that stuff.'

That's what she *might* have said. And, if she had, you know what would have happened. And she knew too. So, she merely remarked that it would make an excellent article for the *North American Review*. In other words, she praised it and at the same time subtly suggested that it wouldn't do as a speech. Lyman Abbott saw the point, tore up his carefully prepared manuscript and preached without even using notes.

POINTS TO REMEMBER

1. Modify your vocabulary to soften the blow of criticism.
2. Never directly address someone's error.
3. If you have to criticize once, praise thrice.

17

IF YOU DON'T DO THIS, YOU ARE HEADED FOR TROUBLE

Sometimes it is difficult to remember a name, particularly if it is hard to pronounce. Rather than even try to learn it, many people ignore it or call the person by an easy nickname. Sid Levy called on a customer for some time whose name was Nicodemus Papadoulos. Most people just called him 'Nick.' Levy told us, 'I made a special effort to say his name over several times to myself before I made my call. When I greeted him by his full name, "Good afternoon, Mr Nicodemus Papadoulos," he was shocked. For what seemed like several minutes there was no reply from him at all. Finally, he said with tears rolling down his cheeks, "Mr Levy, in all the fifteen years I have been in this country, nobody has ever made the effort to call me by my right name."'

What was the reason for Andrew Carnegie's success?

He was called the Steel King; yet he himself knew little about the manufacture of steel. He had hundreds of people working for him who knew far more about steel than he did.

But he knew how to handle people, and that is what made him rich. Early in life, he showed a flair for organisation, a genius for leadership. By the time he was ten, he too had discovered the astounding importance people place on their own name. And he used that discovery to win cooperation. To illustrate: when he was a boy back in Scotland, he got hold of a rabbit, a mother rabbit. Presto! He soon had a whole nest of little rabbits—and nothing to feed them. But he had a brilliant idea. He told the boys and girls in the neighbourhood that if they would go out and pull enough clover and dandelions to feed the rabbits, he would name the bunnies in their honour.

The plan worked like magic, and Carnegie never forgot it.

Years later, he made millions by using the same psychology in business. For example, he wanted to sell steel rails to the Pennsylvania Railroad. J. Edgar Thomson was the president of the Pennsylvania Railroad then. So Andrew Carnegie built a huge steel mill in Pittsburgh and called it the 'Edgar Thomson Steel Works'.

Most people don't remember names, for the simple reason that they don't take the time and energy necessary to concentrate and repeat and fix names indelibly in their minds. They make excuses for themselves; they are too busy.

Napoleon the Third, Emperor of France and nephew of the great Napoleon, boasted that in spite of all his royal duties he could remember the name of every person he met.

His technique? Simple. If he didn't hear the name distinctly, he said, 'So sorry. I didn't get the name clearly.' Then, if it was an unusual name, he would say, 'How is it spelled?'

During the conversation, he took the trouble to repeat the name several times, and tried to associate it in his mind with the person's features, expression and general appearance.

If the person was someone of importance, Napoleon went to even further pains. As soon as His Royal Highness was alone, he wrote the name down on a piece of paper, looked at it, concentrated on it, fixed it securely in his mind and then tore up the paper. In this way, he gained an eye impression of the name as well as an ear impression.

All this takes time, but 'Good manners,' said Emerson, 'are made up of petty sacrifices.'

The importance of remembering and using names is not just the prerogative of kings and corporate executives. It works for all of us. Ken Nottingham, an employee of General Motors in Indiana, usually had lunch at the company cafeteria. He noticed that the woman who worked behind the counter always had a scowl on her face. 'She had been making sandwiches for about two hours and I was just another sandwich to her. I told her what I wanted. She weighed out the ham on a little scale, then she gave me one leaf of lettuce, a few potato chips and handed them to me.

'The next day I went through the same line. Same woman, same scowl. I smiled and said, "Hello, Eunice," and then told her what I wanted. Well, she forgot the scale, piled on the ham, gave me three leaves of lettuce and heaped on the potato chips until they fell off the plate.'

We should be aware of the *magic* contained in a name and realise that this single item is wholly and completely owned by the person with whom we are dealing… and nobody else.

The name sets the individual apart; it makes him or her unique among all others. The information we are imparting or the request we are making takes on a special importance when we approach the situation with the name of the individual. From the waitress to the senior executive, the name will work magic as we deal with others.

POINTS TO REMEMBER

1. The simple secret behind a person's success.
2. An average person is more interested in his or her own name than in all the other names on earth put together.
3. Opt for smart work not hard work.

18

MAKING IT HAPPEN

Look out the window. Notice how much change has occurred out there in just the past few years.

The post-war boom went bust. Competition became global. Consumers grew more sophisticated. Quality became an expectation. Whole new industries were born, and others were realigned. Some dried up and blew away. The idea of two military superpowers now seems like ancient history.

The Eastern Bloc fell apart. Europe is growing more unified by the day. The Third World countries are trying to elbow their way onto the economic stage. Most of the cushiness has gone out of modern capitalism—and with it the blessed stability that generations of business people had come to expect.

Did I anticipate every one of these changes? Of course not. No one could have in a world changing so fast.

But I did possess set of human-relations principles that are just as relevant today as they ever were. And as things turned out, they are uniquely suited to the current high-stress, fast-moving, uncertain world.

1. Look at things from the other person's perspective.
2. Offer genuine appreciation and praise.
3. Harness the mighty power of enthusiasm.

4. Respect the dignity of others.
5. Don't be overly critical.
6. Give people a good reputation to live up to.
7. Keep a sense of fun and balance in your life.

Three generations of students and business people have benefited from this essential wisdom. More people are benefiting every day.

The timelessness of these principles should come as no surprise. They were never rooted in the realities of any particular moment, realities that are guaranteed to change and change. I found that these insights were solid. They merely needed to be applied. They were built around basic facts of human nature, so their essential truth never waned. They worked when the world was humming along. In this new era of constant change, they work just as well. Only now the need for these principles—for anything that works—is greater than it's ever been.

So apply these basic lessons and techniques. Make them part of your daily life. Use them with your friends, family, and colleagues. See what a difference they can make.

These principles don't require an advanced degree in human psychology. They don't call for years of reflection and thought. All they take is practice, energy, and a real desire to get along better in the world.

The rules we have set down here are not mere theories or guesswork about the principles we teach. They work like magic. Incredible as it sounds, I have seen the application of these principles literally revolutionize the lives of many people.

So take those words to heart, and find the leader in you.

POINTS TO REMEMBER

1. Look at things from the other person's perspective.
2. Harness the mighty power of enthusiasm.
3. Keep a sense of fun and balance in your life.